How to Pass a Test

Lynne Edwards

How to Pass a Test
Is this the direction of Australian education today?

How to Pass a Test: Is this the direction of Australian education today
ISBN 978 1 76041 040 7
Copyright © text Lynne Edwards 2015

First published 2015 by
Ginninderra Press
PO Box 3461 Port Adelaide 5015
www.ginninderrapress.com.au

Contents

	Preface: Why Write This Book?	7
1	NAPLAN	11
2	How Children Learn	26
3	The Role of the Teacher	41
4	Valuing Teachers	56
5	The Role of the Parent	75
6	Finland	93
7	Conclusion	107
	Notes	128
	Bibliography	133

Dedicated to my parents Emma and Roy,
two lifelong learners who provided me with inspiration,
encouragement, guidance, support and unconditional love always

Preface

Why Write This Book?

What would a world-famous civil rights leader, a four-year-old child and a group of disheartened professionals have in common? They provided the inspiration and impetus to write this book. I am not an academic or a politician or a professor. I am a classroom teacher with more than thirty years' experience. I know how children learn best, and what is happening in Australian schools now does not demonstrate best practice.

Why write this book? This is the book I wished somebody had written and that I could read, a book that would find an explanation for the direction we have taken in education in recent years; one that would research possible alternatives and offer reassurance about the future of education in our country. I finally moved past the frustration of complaining about the situation and wishing for improvement. My colleagues in Canada were equally perplexed about the trend in Western countries towards the market model driving education reform. Once I began researching, I found it both satisfying and stimulating. Even if nothing was to come of it, it served a purpose. I felt I was doing something constructive, something that might make a difference.

I have always been inspired by Mahatma Gandhi's advice: 'We have to be the change we want to see in the world.' I have encountered too many disheartened, exhausted and unappreciated teachers who have serious concerns for the future of the Australian education system. Hopefully this will support my dedicated colleagues and have a positive influence on those policy-makers who have the power to determine our future direction.

Another motivation came from one of my preschool students from several years ago. This delightful little girl with a Shirley Temple personality, had spina bifida and hadn't been expected to walk. She had a remarkably positive outlook on life. When I asked her how she came to walk, she replied, 'I got sick of being trodden on.' I noticed her photo in the newspaper years later and she had just obtained her pilot's licence to fly.

I should probably also explain the title, *How to Pass a Test*. Sarcasm is not my usual approach, but I seriously questioned, 'Has it really come to this? What has happened to our schools? Is this really the future direction for education in Australia?' I was horrified to see NAPLAN-style testing kits in the post office and supermarket. Not only is NAPLAN testing given a disproportionate amount of time in schools but now parents are being encouraged to further harass their children at home. NAPLAN testing has increasingly overtaken the curriculum. The amount of time and effort involved cannot be justified for the results it reportedly hopes to achieve. This is not the way teachers were trained to teach and it is not the way children learn. As a diagnostic tool, testing can be beneficial. However, once a narrow testing system is given the high stakes status attached to the My School website and then published in league tables, the distortion becomes detrimental and destructive.

Governments have not made evidence-based decisions and have chosen to impose systems that have failed in the UK and USA. The overemphasis on standardised testing has led to a narrowing of the curriculum. The focus has been redirected to content and delivery rather than providing children with a meaningful, comprehensive education that will serve them well in life.

I will structure my argument by identifying the limitations of NAPLAN; its ineffectiveness as a performance tool; and the high stakes associated with the My School website and the associated league tables. In contrast, I will follow with an examination of how children really learn. This will lead to a discussion of the teacher's role and will demonstrate the complexities involved in teaching and learning, and the importance of valuing teachers. The other component of successful learning, the parent's role, will follow. I will then elaborate on one of the most successful education systems that we could emulate – that of Finland. I will conclude with an analysis of successful education systems and a discussion of the possible future direction of education in Australia.

I would like to thank the many educators and parents who have discussed this issue with me and have provided insight and support for the concept of this book.

1

NAPLAN

When considering introducing a program to an education system, policy-makers need to ask obvious questions. What need does it serve? How is it to be evaluated to assess whether it has achieved its purpose?

The National Assessment Program – Literacy and Numeracy (NAPLAN), an annual assessment testing system for students in Years 3, 5, 7, and 9, was introduced in Australia in 2008. The intention behind introducing NAPLAN had some merit; however, the way it was administered and interpreted has proven counterproductive. It was designed as a diagnostic or measurement tool to determine whether students are meeting educational outcomes in literacy and numeracy. It was intended to test how effective current educational programs are, and to identify priorities for improvement. Individual student performance scores were to be made available so parents could compare their child's results to those of the national average.

Unfortunately, the process and the results have become seriously flawed. There were unintended but entirely predictable consequences. NAPLAN has influenced teaching methods and led to teaching to the test. It has dominated and narrowed the curriculum. It presents an unreliable and very limited picture of a student's development, and professionals have found that conclusions based on NAPLAN results are erroneous, inaccurate and misleading.

Professor Margaret Wu, Principal Research Fellow at Melbourne University, with a background in educational measurement and statistics, has exposed systematic errors in the analysis of NAPLAN testing and data. Her work has revealed large margins of error in measuring performance. She has warned, 'When comparative results are presented we have to determine whether the differences in scores are due to random fluctuations or genuine differences,' and she adds, 'The publication of NAPLAN results at the school level will do great harm to Australian education because of the complexities of the interpretation of results.'[1]

Professor Wu points out that NAPLAN data does not represent a realistic or comprehensive reflection of students' progress. The tests are based on forty questions administered once a year for two subject areas, literacy and numeracy. They do not take into account student ability, natural talent or success in any other curriculum subjects. They do not measure abilities such as creative thinking skills, integrity, resilience, motivation, application of knowledge or the ability to analyse and solve problems; all skills necessary for successful learning. NAPLAN testing is not even significant as a diagnostic tool because of the time gap between the testing period in May and the feedback which is provided much later in the year.

Ultimately, NAPLAN testing has not produced a realistic and comprehensive snapshot of education today. The test results have assumed disproportionate significance and have a pivotal influence on the My School website, the resulting league tables and will shortly also be a major determinant of teacher performance pay.

> 'Children have more need of models than critics.'
> – Joseph Joubert

Teaching to the test, cheating and narrowing of the curriculum

Both overseas and locally, problems have arisen when school funding is tied to high-stakes literacy and numeracy tests, and this inevitably leads to 'teaching to the test'. It is logical to assume that other important aspects of the curriculum are sacrificed when so much time is devoted to preparation for NAPLAN testing. Time taken away from regular programs is focused on a narrow range of topics with the express purpose of achieving the best possible test results.

Media reports imply some teachers have left charts on walls and have encouraged poorly-performing students to stay away on test days.

NAPLAN testing has come to dominate school life to the extent that teachers in Year 2 are preparing their students for particular text types and genres that are to be tested the next year, whether they are relevant to the diverse needs of the students or not.

The Australian Curriculum, Assessment and Reporting Authority (ACRA) is aware of the prevalence of cheating, and its occurrence 'continues to flourish after twenty or more years of publication of school results and league tables in the US and England'.[2] In fact, these countries are now reversing the over-testing trend, and are recognising that similar test-based programs – such as the USA's No Child Left Behind, and Race To the Top – have failed in their objective to raise student achievement. With complaints of turning schools into testing factories, and with vast numbers of schools stigmatised as failing schools due to unrealistic goals, they are looking for a new direction.

In fact, here in Australia a whole industry has been built around NAPLAN as a result of the focus and importance attached to testing. NAPLAN test booklets are available in newsagents and supermarkets. Organisations are offering NAPLAN tutoring and workshops. Education department websites advertise 'persuasive writing' workshops in line with the current genre being tested. A television advertisement linking a children's Omega3 supplement to success in the NAPLAN tests was only withdrawn after social media protest. In schools, special NAPLAN classes have been created to coach those less likely to succeed in the tests. Professional development providers such as David Hornsby have demonstrated alarm at receiving requests from teaching staff specifying 'NAPLAN training'.[3] At the same time, we have seen the demise of interest in hiring curriculum consultants in all other areas, such as science, the arts, drama and music. Professor Robin Alexander of Cambridge University concluded, 'the narrowing of the curriculum may have actually reduced overall standards and robbed children of their right to a broad and balanced curriculum'.[4]

Understandably, accompanying the focus on NAPLAN testing is an increase in stress levels for both staff and students. In fact, the term 'NAPLAN belly' has been coined to describe a common ailment during the testing period. In a survey commissioned by the University of Western Sydney's Whitlam Institute, teachers reported students displaying symptoms of stress including crying, vomiting, insomnia and absenteeism during NAPLAN testing.[5] The report concluded, 'Although NAPLAN testing is designed to improve the quality of education children and young people receive in Australia, its implementation, uses and misuses mean that it undermines quality education, and it does harm that is not in the best interest of Australian children.' When an education minister defends the testing regime with comments such as 'If schools and teachers teach NAPLAN in the way it is intended there is no reason at all why this should be extra pressure on kids in the classroom.'[6] The use of the words 'teach NAPLAN' implies that NAPLAN is thought as a subject to be taught, and it demonstrates how the test itself has come to dominate the curriculum.

ACRA, the agency in charge of national literacy and numeracy tests, suggested in a submission to a Senate enquiry in June 2013 that teachers and principals are responsible for creating stress among students. Yet the blame lies squarely with the high stakes attached to NAPLAN testing. That fact is pivotal to the detrimental effects of the testing regime. NAPLAN results should never have been published. They should have been used simply as a diagnostic tool. However, as Maurie Mulheron the president of the NSW Teachers Federation pointed out, 'As soon as you publish the results on a website and allow immediate access to them, it turns into an adult spectator sport.'[7]

Pasi Sahlberg, Director General of the Ministry of Education in Finland advises, 'Creative learning can only be created and maintained in places that are close to fear-free.

Used with permission of Cathy Wilcox.

Negative anxiety and fear down-shift the mind; kill creativity and prevent risk taking.'[8] Our 'reform' agendas are in stark contrast to those of the highly successful Finnish system that he represents.[9]

Many of the parents who think the My School website and associated league tables are helpful are uninformed of the limited value of the tests. It has not been explained or clarified for them that these results do not represent a complete or accurate reflection of a school's performance. The results are inadequate, narrow and skewed because of the high stakes attached to them.

Testing and other forms of assessment

Of course we need to assess how children learn. However, testing is not the only or best method of evaluation. Many would argue that in some cases testing creates stress and anxiety that interferes with and restricts a student's ability to perform at his or her best. In fact, John Simons, Arts Dean of Macquarie University, has advocated no exams. He believes students perform better with other forms of assessment. In a statement he added, 'Students would probably achieve more of their potential if they were freed from the pressure of examinations.'[10]

Excessive testing is counter-productive. You have to question the validity of the exam experience of memorising as much information as possible and regurgitating it later. How much long-term knowledge and deep meaning is retained from such methods? Testing is also a single measurement taken on a particular day and is affected by many variables such as whether the student is ill, anxious or, for whatever reason, not performing at his best. Tests should be a small part of a comprehensive, realistic evaluation of progress. Other valid forms of assessment do not come at such a cost. A more useful and relevant form of comprehensive assessment is regularly undertaken in classrooms.

Professor Brian Caldwell, managing director of consulting group Educational Transformations, acknowledged that before NAPLAN was introduced, Australian schools already demonstrated outstanding professional practice, with continual monitoring and assessment of student's progress. In a Senate enquiry into NAPLAN in 2010, he advocated that the program and the website should be phased out.[11]

Standardised tests have been in place in some states for twenty years and national tests have been conducted since 1999.[12] They were useful diagnostic tools. The significant difference with NAPLAN testing is that NAPLAN, with all its flaws, is attached to high stakes accountability through the My School website and accompanying league tables.

The nostalgic call for 'back to basics' assumes that since schools developed a more comprehensive curriculum they have abandoned the three Rs. Nothing could be further from the truth.

Teachers have become so much more accountable in recent years and education systems more transparent. It is true that class sizes were larger in the 1950s and 60s but teaching methods were vastly different. Students were streamed for ease of instruction and

3rd in class

Half-Yearly Examination June, 1962

Subject	Mark	Class Average	Subject	Mark	Class Average
Reading	87	75	English	66	64.3
Composition	83	73	Art	C	D
Spelling	90	79	Handcrafts	C	D
Writing	C	D	Science and Health	C	D
Arithmetic	262/300	219/300	Music	D	D
Social Studies	70	64	Physical Education	D	D

Days absent 0   Conduct *Good*

Class % = 72%
Pupil % = 83%

A very satisfactory worker. English could have been better.

R. Carey
Class Teacher

Third place in Class
I am pleased,
Lynne!

M. J. Keating
Head Teacher

Parent *E. Carradine*

All marks are allotted out of a total of 100.
Please return to class teacher on first day of next term.

the whole class was lectured to with the same educational material irrespective of whether students were slow learners or gifted. Reports consisted of test results and a scant comment from the teacher, usually satisfactory or unsatisfactory. I was Little Miss Average, as my Grade Two report shows. My parents rarely had personal interviews with my teachers and as long as there was no trouble they probably assumed all was fine.

When I became a teacher, the whole landscape had changed dramatically. In today's schools, students are monitored and assessed on an individual basis using a variety of formats and assessment tools. Teachers use a series of detailed checklists, anecdotal records, set assignments, portfolios of examples of work, regular testing of various methods and extensive reports. There is the expectation that teachers should have a thorough knowledge of each of their pupils. Individual learning programs (ILPs) are devised, regular parent teacher interviews are arranged and parents are extremely well informed of their child's progress. Before finalising reports, teachers of the same year level collaborate using a moderation process whereby they compare the results of students from different classes. They agree on a standard measurement for grading that ensures a consistency of judgement across the classes, thereby limiting subjectivity. In the chapter on the teacher's role, I elaborate on student assessment, and the high standards expected of teachers.

The current obsession with standardised testing does not provide a true reflection of a child's ability. In life, it is only in the school situation where we are grouped together with people of the same age, and this is mainly for the convenience of those who are organising us. When we enter the workforce, we mix with people of all ages and backgrounds and we are not compared with others in age groupings. We are judged on our efficiency and productivity.

Society does not expect all babies to achieve their milestones of rolling over, sitting, crawling, walking and talking each at the same time. As well, parents accept that if a baby is putting all her energy into crawling, she may not necessarily be learning lots of new words at the same time. When babies achieve a milestone, parents celebrate their success and provide the greatest accolades and encouragement. By demonstrating such approval and providing enthusiastic encouragement, the babies continue to thrive.

The most meaningful and realistic evaluation of a student's performance and development is the measurement of his improvement compared with his own previous record and the amount of effort he exerted. Even professional athletes focus on their 'personal best'. Considering each individual's different circumstances, it is somewhat irrelevant to compare one student to another. It can be helpful to have an awareness of expected milestones but the importance attached to NAPLAN results is simply misplaced.

Literacy and numeracy are the core business of schools. However, to claim or imply that the NAPLAN results are a true or complete representation of how a school is travelling is misleading. Then to use those results to compare school performance in the My School website and in league tables for the purpose of informing parents and influencing their decisions over school choice is misguided. As Jane Caro, education consultant and lecturer at the University of Western Sydney, rightly reminds us on the issue of choice: education is about the children, not the parents.

My School website and league tables

When introducing NAPLAN and the My School website, the government of the day made unfounded assumptions that parents were not well informed about their child's progress. They repeatedly stated that parents have the right to know and that there was need for more transparency. I don't recall anyone asking parents what they want or expect, or making any effort to ensure that parents understand what is being presented. Politicians have simply made assumptions about what people want. In addition, the Australian Education Union (AEU) in a submission to a Senate enquiry in November 2010 agreed that parents have a right to know about their children's progress. However, they pointed out, 'there is no inherent right to information concerning other children in the school'.[13]

The government published NAPLAN results on the My School website believing it would create pressures for school improvement and inform parents about school choice. Used as a diagnostic tool, test results can be useful. However, as I have already demonstrated, NAPLAN results do not represent a true or complete reflection of students' or schools' achievements and are susceptible to misinterpretation. They should never have been published. In fact, Professor Margaret Wu issued a challenge to government. 'Publicly name an underperforming school based on NAPLAN results.' She added, 'They won't because common sense tells them it's an inadequate and inaccurate picture.'[14]

One of the stated intentions was to identify schools that needed assistance and to allocate funding appropriately. The irony that resulted was that parents were encouraged to use the My School website to compare schools and make choices. They left the schools most in need, those identified as under-performing, thus compounding the problems and difficulties associated with these schools.

A colleague at a local primary school, commenting on feedback from one of his student's parents, noted that the parent was impressed with the NAPLAN results of the Year 3 students. That particular cohort was reasonably competent and their results were pleasing. However, the teacher was much more impressed with and proud of the Year 5 results because they had demonstrated greater improvement in all of their assessment formats.

Using the My School website, we now have media-compiled league tables. This has created the extremely damaging situation of winners and losers amongst schools. The emerging drift to better-resourced schools has resulted in a greater divide in society between the haves and the have nots. When you do not have a broad social mix in schools, the less well-resourced schools are left with a disproportionate number of students with high level needs, and naturally it is more difficult to achieve positive results. Obviously, children with English as a second language would learn more effectively when mixing with good role models. The issue of parental choice is often quoted when considering and comparing schools, but realistically, what choice do the parents of an Aboriginal child from Alice Springs, for example, have when determining whether they might send their child to Kings College in Sydney? The reality is that this philosophy is creating a greater social divide within the Australian community. As Chris Bonner and Jane

Caro warn, in their book *The Stupid Country*, 'It is in all our interests to increase the prosperity of everyone, and no one recognises this more acutely than the business people who need skilled workers to compete successfully in world markets.'[15]

> There must be such a thing as a child with average ability, but you can't find a parent who will admit that it is his child.'
> – Thomas Bailey

Teacher performance pay

Unfortunately, both sides of politics in Australia favour the introduction of teacher performance pay despite overwhelming evidence that such schemes have failed overseas. A recent RAND Corporation study of three US teacher performance pay schemes in New York, Nashville and Texas found 'paying teachers to improve student performance did not lead to increases in student achievements and did not change what teachers did in their classrooms relative to the control groups in any of the three experiments'.[16] Similar findings and comments resulted from a study by the National Bureau of Economic Research, noting, 'Performance pay schemes operating in Iowa, Texas, Chicago, Denver and Nashville school districts have all been evaluated recently and found not to have improved student results.'[17] The Australian government based our new direction in education on Joel Klein's New York program. The New York City Education Department is now abandoning the School Wide Performance Bonus Program (SPBP). Unfortunately often initiatives are based on assumptions rather than evidence.

As predictable as teaching to the test followed the introduction of NAPLAN testing, the practice would be reinforced if it was to be a major determinant of teacher bonuses. As Diane Ravitch from New York University concluded, 'Thus far, there is a paucity of evidence that paying teachers to raise test scores leads to anything other than teaching to the test.'[18] The introduction of teacher performance pay will not achieve its stated objectives for the following reasons.

Teaching is a profession which requires dedication and devotion.

People who are attracted to it are certainly not drawn principally by the current salary on offer. Those who try teaching and decide they're not suited to it leave. To remain in such a demanding, all-consuming profession would be detrimental to both the students and the teacher concerned. Teachers therefore are not primarily motivated by salary and conditions. They receive intrinsic rewards through the satisfaction of making a difference. An appropriate salary would be appreciated but money is not the prime motivator.

The collegiate nature of teaching does not fit well with such a competitive and divisive scheme. Teachers share information, consult and support each other in the interests of their students. They have a united, egalitarian approach. Team-teaching requires a great deal of collaborative planning and cooperation. As an example, I recently noticed a sign on a staffroom notice board entitled Teaching Networks and Supports. Evaluations of failed teacher performance pay schemes noted that where there was unequal disbursement of bonuses, unsurprisingly it resulted in disharmony and resentment. It is not always the most deserving teachers but the most effective self-promoters who are successful recipients of bonuses.

To offer performance bonuses is too simplistic an approach for an incredibly complex issue. Measurement is not as straightforward as, for example, in the car sales or real-estate industry. The more cars or houses you sell, obviously the more successful you are and bonuses are awarded accordingly. However, in teaching it would be extremely difficult to measure, unless of course you based it on NAPLAN results. It has already been demonstrated how inadequate they are as a complete assessment tool.

To demonstrate the inadequacy of using NAPLAN results as a measurement of success, let's consider the reality of its administration. When NAPLAN testing occurs in May each year, the current teacher has been teaching that particular class for just over three months. How much influence has the teacher from the previous year had on those students? How would you measure that? How do you prove the effectiveness of one particular teacher?

In high schools, a teacher might have a maths class of gifted students one year and a class of challenged or low-achieving students the next year. Is he deemed to be a failure then based on the scores of his class? Or if the situation was reversed would that be perceived as a remarkable improvement in his performance?

Within the school community it is well-known that cohorts of students pass through each year and they may be predominantly successful or otherwise. It depends on many variables including their socio-economic background, the level of support they receive from home, and their different needs such as English as a second language (ESL). Teachers obviously make a difference and use all their skills to assist students. However, often it takes more than one year to achieve a significant difference. A student's performance and success are not dependent only on his teacher's talent.

Professor Helen Ladd is a US academic researcher with experience in longitudinal studies of education. She notes, 'For both teachers and principals it is neither fair nor constructive to try to hold them accountable for factors over which they have little control, using statistical measures that are based on a narrow range of outcomes, and that are subject to large amounts of variability.' She adds, 'Year comparisons are inappropriate because of the changing mix of students from year to year,' and 'even the most sophisticated approaches typically cannot distinguish the contribution of teachers from the classroom context.'[19]

It is interesting to note that when new governments have to explain a set of poor figures, they blame the previous government. Yet this principle does not appear to apply when it comes to judging teachers and their influence on students.

The prospect of encouraging teachers to 'try harder' with the offer of performance pay is not a realistic incentive. Teaching is not a job where you can put in a half-hearted effort. The point is that most teachers are already offering their best. How can you give more than your most? Geoff Masters, from the Australian Council for Educational Research (ACER) noted, 'Results-based incentive schemes have a disappointing track record' because they 'ignore the research on human motivation.' He refers to evidence from psychology 'that paying people for things they would have done anyway can lower performance'.[20]

If schools are penalised based on NAPLAN results and are categorised as under-performing, teachers would theoretically be encouraged to seek environments where it is easier to teach, and therefore attract performance bonuses. The irony is that exceptional teachers are the very ones needed in disadvantaged schools. Even if students in these schools have achieved remarkable individual improvements based on their previous record and due to their own and their teacher's efforts, they will, with standardised testing, be classified as under-performing and therefore not rewarded.

As to the question of assessing which teachers would qualify for a bonus: where there are improvements in student achievement, how would you determine or prove it was directly attributed to the teacher performance bonus incentive or a combination of factors? In what time frame would it be judged? If performance pay is to be closely tied to NAPLAN results, the process would be meaningless. Multiple performance measures would need to be factored in. Proposed measures include teacher observation, parent feedback, teacher qualifications, professional development and contribution to extra-curricular activities. This would obviously require a tremendous amount of time and energy devoted to teacher assessment. This is time taken away from teaching in the classroom. As has been demonstrated in the USA, this is a very costly administrative process. Given that performance bonuses failed to achieve improved performances from students, it would be a waste of taxpayers' money estimated to be 1.25 billion dollars over five years.[21] Clearly this has not been thought through. 'Teacher Performance Pay is not the magic bullet that so often the policy world is looking for.'[22]

Conclusion

The combination of NAPLAN testing, the My School website and the league tables, along with the prospect of teacher performance pay, has had negative consequences for the Australian education system. There is now a narrow focus in the school curriculum. A major emphasis has become teaching to the test, and parents do not have an accurate snapshot of how their children or schools are progressing.

The Director of the Whitlam Institute, Eric Sidoti, when referring to the survey on the negative effects of NAPLAN (conducted in 2012), concluded, 'The report suggests the NAPLAN testing regime is plagued with unintended consequences well beyond its stated intent. It does represent a shift to high-stakes testing.'[23] He also noted, 'It's time to open the debate. We need to ensure that the development of literacy and numeracy in our schools is assessed and reported in a way that enhances rather than constrains pedagogy, that evokes confidence and enthusiasm among educators rather than resignation; that challenges and encourages learning rather than induces widespread anxiety and stress among students.'[24]

An August 2015 review of NAPLAN results 'showed that in the seven years since the tests were introduced in primary and high schools, most measurements showed no major improvement'. What does this tell us? The tests were designed to identify problems and enable teachers to reflect and adapt programs to achieve greater success. Given that the test results are far from comprehensive or accurate, perhaps they demonstrate the inadequacies of the testing regime.

A 2015 segment of John Oliver's social commentary *Last Week Tonight* highlighted the level of saturation of standardised testing in the US education system, particularly in relation to the Common Core program. He revealed bizarre advertisements that are used to convince students that testing is fun, and official instructions that are provided to administrators detailing procedures for when a child vomits during an exam. After years of standardised testing, higher education standards have not been achieved. Oliver asks the poignant question, 'If students and teachers are not gaining anything from standardised testing, then who is benefiting from the system?' He suggests that the large corporations such as Pearson Education which prepare, administer and provide evaluation of the tests, despite frequent errors and shortcomings in grading procedures, continue to enjoy growth and profit and remain a dominant force in education.

A famous old cartoon succinctly illustrates the fallacy of standardised testing. A bird, a monkey, a penguin, an elephant, a goldfish in a bowl, a seal and a dog are lined up under a tree. They are instructed by an examiner, 'For a fair selection, everybody has to take the same exam. Please climb that tree.' The cartoon was inspired by a quote attributed to Albert Einstein: 'Everybody is a genius. But if you judge a fish by its ability to climb a tree, it will live its whole life believing it is stupid.'

In the following chapter, I examine the complexities of how children learn effectively, which is in stark contrast to the current emphasis on standardised testing.

2

How Children Learn

> 'Give a man a fish and you feed him for a day. Teach a man to fish and you feed him for a lifetime.' – Chinese proverb

Because of my background, my focus will be on how children learn during the early-childhood years, the most formative and influential years. Many of the fundamental principles of learning apply throughout life.

To understand how children learn, the obvious place to start is at the beginning. Research has shown that babies know a lot more than most people would be aware of. I will be discussing how young children use their senses to discover the world about them, how they learn through play, and the significance and relevance of the arts. I will be investigating the importance of movement in learning, and the significance of establishing a foundation to determine learning readiness. I will outline the different learning styles, and investigate what is known of brain plasticity and the dilemmas associated with learning difficulties.

A definition of learning

What is learning? Is it a matter of accumulating as many facts as possible, or is there more to it? Facts are readily available via the internet at any time. We don't expect anyone to know everything there is to know, but if children have the interest, motivation and tools to learn, they can succeed in the world. Children need to learn how to independently investigate and search for information, how to assess its relevance and how to apply it in a meaningful way. Those who have a supportive home background that encourages, inspires and provides motivation for continuous, lifelong learning have a distinct advantage.

> 'Education is not the filling of a pail, but the lighting of a fire.' – William Butler Yeats

Beginning with babies

'Walk upstairs, open the door gently, and look in the crib. What do you see? Most of us see a picture of innocence and helplessness, a clean slate. But, in fact, what we see in the crib is the greatest mind that has ever existed, the most powerful learning machine in the universe. The tiny fingers and mouth are exploration devices that probe the alien world around them with more precision than any Mars rover. The crumpled ears take a buzz of incomprehensible noise and flawlessly turn it into meaningful language. The wide eyes that sometimes seem to peer into your very soul actually do just that, deciphering your deepest feelings. The downy head surrounds a brain that is forming millions of new connections every day. That, at least, is what thirty years of scientific research have told us.'[1]

When I first read that passage from *The Scientist in the Crib*, I was captivated. In 2003 I was researching for MiniQ, Questacon's permanent exhibition for babies to six-year-olds when I discovered this wonderful resource; an inspirational, informative book that chronicled a study of how we learn. The authors, Alison Gobnic, Andrew Meltzoff and Patricia Kuhl are psychologists who have been scientifically researching cognitive development in children. Over a number of years, they devised ingenious techniques to observe and interpret what babies know and how they learn. Their research demonstrates that a great deal of learning begins well before school. In fact, it seems babies recognise their mother's voice at birth possibly due to 'the muted but still audible sounds they hear in the womb'.[2]

Babies do not begin as a blank slate. The authors of *The Scientist in the Crib* refer to three elements of knowledge: 'innate knowledge, powerful learning abilities and unconscious tuition from adults'.[3]

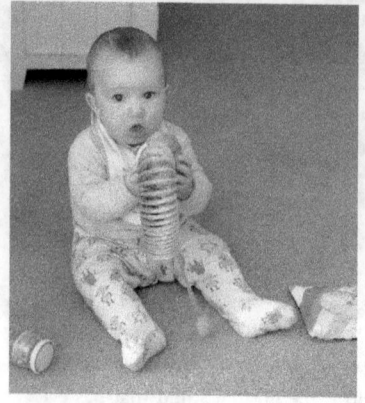

Newborns can discriminate between human faces and voices and other sights and sounds, and they prefer them. Within the first nine months, they become aware of and relate to emotions. They can differentiate between expressions of happiness, sadness and anger.

Initially babies across all cultures babble in an identical way experimenting with consonant and vowel combinations. Interestingly, the baby words for mother and father are similar across cultures, with variations of mama and papa or dada. Each language is unique. However, very young babies can discriminate the sounds of different languages. They are virtually 'universal linguists'. After exposure to their own culture, they lose the ability to 'hear' sounds that are not regularly used in their own language. For example, Japanese adults find it difficult to differentiate between the sounds of l and r, and Australians find it difficult to reproduce the guttural inflections used in many European languages.

'Learning to understand a language is like cracking a deeply encrypted code. We all crack this code effortlessly and at an age we can't even remember.'[4] Babies are able to turn a continuous stream of sounds into meaningful words, using their innate knowledge and exceptional learning abilities. However, parents play a crucial role. They are designed to help babies learn. When they intuitively engage in 'motherese' or 'baby talk', parents enhance their babies' learning opportunities. Everybody would be aware of how parents address their babies in a manner noticeably different from how they interact with other adults. When engaging with their babies, parents raise the pitch of their voices and accentuate vowels slowly and clearly in a playful and melodic manner 'Howzzz my cuute little babeeee?'; and babies respond accordingly. Their attention is immediately captured. They come to understand the interactive nature of language, and over time they learn to attach meaning to words.

Babies' achievements are much more complicated than the capabilities of computers. They actively engage in scientific methods by continuously searching for patterns and testing hypotheses. They seem to have a need or an innate drive to find out and seek explanations. 'The apparently pointless activities we call play often seem to be the result of this drive.'[5] Through games of imitation and hide and seek, they learn about their ever expanding world. 'By the time they are in kindergarten, children have mastered almost all of the complexities of their particular language, with no conscious effort or instruction.'[6]

Learning through the senses

As demonstrated in the discussion on how babies learn, the senses are of major significance when considering how children learn. Children assimilate knowledge and explore their environment using the senses of sight, sound, touch, smell and taste. Babies in particular absorb a lot of information through the largest organ of the body, the skin. Their level of comfort and therefore contentedness depends on their surroundings. If they are warm and wrapped snugly, that adds to their security. They also place great emphasis on oral stimulation, and learn about their surroundings by putting everything within reach in their mouths.

Good hearing and vision are vital for successful learning. However, it is not simply a matter of whether the eyes and ears are functioning properly. Visual and auditory processing is of vital significance. The connection between the eyes and the brain, and the ears and the brain, determines how children process and interpret the messages received. The scientist and rehabilitation physician Paul Bach-y Rita has demonstrated that we see with our brains, not with our eyes: 'our eyes merely sense changes in light energy; it is our brains that perceive and hence see'.[7]

Given a stimulating environment and supportive encouragement, children thrive. However, if their development is interrupted at a critical period this could impact significantly on their learning. In his discussion on brain plasticity, Norman Doidge referred to the research of David Hubel and Torsten Wiesel, who were working with kittens to learn how vision is processed. These scientists discovered that there was a 'critical period from the third to the eighth week of life when the newborn kitten's brain had to receive visual stimulation to develop normally'.[8] If the vision of one eye was obstructed during the critical period, the kitten was left blind in that eye for life. The 'visual areas in the brain map that normally processed input from the shut eye had failed to develop'. However, they then discovered that those areas of the brain that had been deprived of stimulation began to process visual input from the unaffected eye and that the brain had effectively rewired itself.

Language development also 'has a critical period that begins in infancy and ends between eight years and puberty'.[9] After this critical period, 'a person's ability to learn a second language without an accent is limited' and in fact is 'not even processed in the same part of the brain as is the native tongue'.

Auditory processing involves hearing, the passive reception of sound; and listening, the processing and interpretation of the information you hear. Good listening skills require concentration, uninterrupted processing and storing of information; and interpreting and retrieving that information. This of course has a significant impact on memory.

> 'It is not the answer that enlightens, but the question.'
> – Eugene Ionesco

Learning through play

Some might think it flippant to claim that children learn through play. But that's exactly what they do. Play is not a matter of time-wasting. It is vital to a child's development.

There are several different theories about play. Mary Sheridan believes play provides the distinct functions of 'apprenticeship, research, occupational therapy and recreation' and that children learn about the world around them 'through a process of observing, exploring, speculating and making discoveries'.[10] As they socialise, children pass through stages of development, beginning with solitary play, then moving on to parallel play, where they demonstrate an awareness of others, and finally maturing to a more cooperative style of interactive play.

Through play, children are experimenting with life. In role-play situations, they are trying out what it might feel like to 'be Daddy'. One kindergarten boy once told me when he grows up he wants to be Daddy so he could get to pick the videos. What he was expressing was a desire to have control over his life, to experience some degree of power. In successful children's books, the heroes are always children. That satisfies the desire to have more choice in their lives. Of course they have to wait to grow up before they're mature enough to handle the responsibilities of adulthood, but in the meantime they like to practise.

To explain and highlight the relevance of play, let's look at what is happening when children play in the bath with jugs, funnels and tubes. As they pour water from small containers to larger containers, they are experimenting with volume and capacity. Repeated experiences confirm and consolidate their theories and their abilities to estimate. They come to conclusions about the size of vessels, their buoyancy, and how surface tension allows water molecules to hold together just above the surface before it spills over. It's all fun, but at the same time they are internalising and comprehending important scientific concepts in a manner that is meaningful and relevant to them.

In May 2012, Play for Life and Play Australia hosted .the inaugural Australian Children's Play Summit in Melbourne. At this event, children from local schools were invited to participate and to contribute their ideas. Feedback indicated they felt more satisfied with playground equipment and activities that were challenging in a 'safe-scary' way. The event highlighted that play is a vital component to children's development and it is recognised in the United Nations Rights of the Child in Article 31.

The importance of the arts

> 'It is the supreme art of the teacher to awaken joy in creative expression and knowledge.' – Albert Einstein

To ensure that children remain engaged in their learning, the most successful methods at primary and high school level involve interactive programs. With the current over-emphasis on standardised testing in education, many are lamenting the loss of a comprehensive and meaningful curriculum. With high stakes attached to a narrow focus, the basics, as the only measurement of success, there is less time and energy devoted to other important elements of a child's education. The arts have diminished in importance. However, occasionally you encounter rare glimmers of hope and insight.

In March 2011, the Sydney Theatre Company's artistic directors, Cate Blanchet and Andrew Upton, launched Professor Robyn Ewing's program The Art and Australian Education: Realising Potential. This is a primary school program that demonstrates how drama is a powerful medium for teaching literacy. Experienced actors working in classrooms alongside teachers have shown that actively engaging students in learning has produced 'improved student literacy outcomes'. Professor Ewing stated, 'The school drama program exemplifies how teaching a specific Arts discipline, in this case drama, can provide a powerful base for transformative learning.' She added that international research shows, 'when students' learning is embedded in the Arts it improves their school performance and attendance'. She also warned that 'achieving the demonstrated educational and social benefits of Arts in education will require a change in thinking by policy makers to ensure that cultivation, imagination and creativity became the priorities rather than the add-ons'.[11]

Sir Ken Robinson, PhD, an internationally-recognised leader in in the field of education, creativity and innovation, and author of The Element, would agree. He does not advocate the production-line mentality of standardised testing and narrowing of the curriculum. He highly values the arts and the development of creative, divergent thinking. In his writings, Sir Ken demonstrates that children begin with creativity but our education system robs them of it. He holds that art, music and drama are as important as science, mathematics, literacy and physical education. Our culture of institutions does not encourage collaboration which produces the best results. He warns that leaders of industry indicate they need people who can think creatively, and can demonstrate flexibility and adaptability in order to cope with the demands and challenges of today's society.[12]

Richard Gill, the music director of Victorian Opera and advocate of music education, also agrees. In his article 'Wake up, Australia, or we'll have a nation of unimaginative robots',[13] he states, 'Activities used for teaching the national tests destroy individuality and stifle creativity.' He strongly believes, 'The very things that promote literacy and numeracy are the arts, beginning with serious arts education in the early years. If we want a creative nation, an imaginative nation, a thinking nation and a nation of individuals, then we must increase the time for arts education, especially music education.' To elaborate, he explains that music education requires 'an extraordinarily high level of listening and concentration' and of 'abstract thinking', and this practice gives children advantages in other areas of learning. In other words, the skills that are nurtured through music education also benefit literacy and numeracy.

Gill strongly believes, 'NAPLAN tests and My School have nothing to do with the education of a child. This abhorred and insidious method of assessing children, teachers and their schools needs to stop now. Principals, teachers and parents need to stand up and be counted, and resist this unnatural activity.'[14]

Movement and learning

The late Barbara Pheloung, from the program Move To Learn, believed that movement is the key to improved academic achievement.[15] Developmental delays are often due to neurological immaturities or retained reflexes from babyhood. These reflexes are an automatic function of newborns, but as the higher brain develops, they are no longer needed. If for any reason these reflexes are retained and remain dominant, the nervous system will react inappropriately and can adversely affect development and learning. Movement activates the neural wiring throughout the body and Pheloung observed that the traditional approach of remedial tutoring, or repeating activities that children with learning difficulties are already failing in, was not only frustrating them but was not enhancing their development. She designed a set of simple movement exercises that have proven to assist with learning.

Children are naturally active. It is quite unfair to ask young children or even adults to sit for extended periods and expect they will remain actively engaged. As young children grow, they master physical skills sequentially through sensory-motor activity. They learn to roll, sit, crawl and walk. Crawling involves coordinating the hands and knees, and mastering crawling indicates a vital stage of integration of the brain. The significance of crawling goes beyond the obvious coordination of both sides of the body. It also helps the eyes to focus on the floor at about the same distance the eyes focus on a book: the reading distance.

Children need many opportunities and lots of practice with play equipment to master the coordination required for walking, running, catching and throwing. By the time they enter school, most have decided on a hand preference and should be able to demonstrate that both sides of the body and brain are working together efficiently.

Body awareness, and proprioception or position-in-space, are vital for learning readiness. Children need to develop an automatic awareness of the position of their limbs and be able to coordinate them with ease. For example, for the skills involved in driving, adults need to automatically coordinate the pedals and steering wheel of a car while simultaneously focusing on the road and other traffic. When children experience difficulty with balance and coordination, they often encounter learning difficulties. If they cannot differentiate left and right and position in space, they often become confused with reading bs and ds and ps and qs.

The vestibular system also incorporates movement and gravity and it affects our sense of balance, coordination and eye movements. The working mechanisms of the inner ear tell us when we are upright and how gravity is affecting our body and our eyes assist us with the understanding of where we are in space; by referencing horizontal lines.

Movement and activity continue to directly relate to learning success throughout life. Professor Dick Telford of the ANU, Research Director of the Lifestyles of Our Kids (LOOK) project, believes being physically active and having a well-rounded approach to education enhances scholastic achievement. In a media release, he stated, 'Research shows that physical activity programs such as Blue Earth are important because of the intimate relationship between the developing body and mind of every child.' Such programs, as well as benefiting physical health 'assist with the learning process in the classroom'. Teachers from the pilot program reported Blue Earth had a positive impact on students' academic performance. This is backed up by evidence from Daniel Siegel, a physician and clinical professor of psychiatry who found that 'Aerobic exercise seems to benefit not only our musculoskeletal systems, but our nervous system as well. We learn more effectively when we are physically active.'[16]

Stages of development and learning readiness

It takes common sense to recognise that children need to master basic skills before attempting to understand more complex skills. Yet our education system sometimes demands children in the same year level should all achieve the same benchmarks at the same time. It would appear to be structured for ease of management rather than the real needs of children.

Learning readiness is a combination of complex skills. Individuals

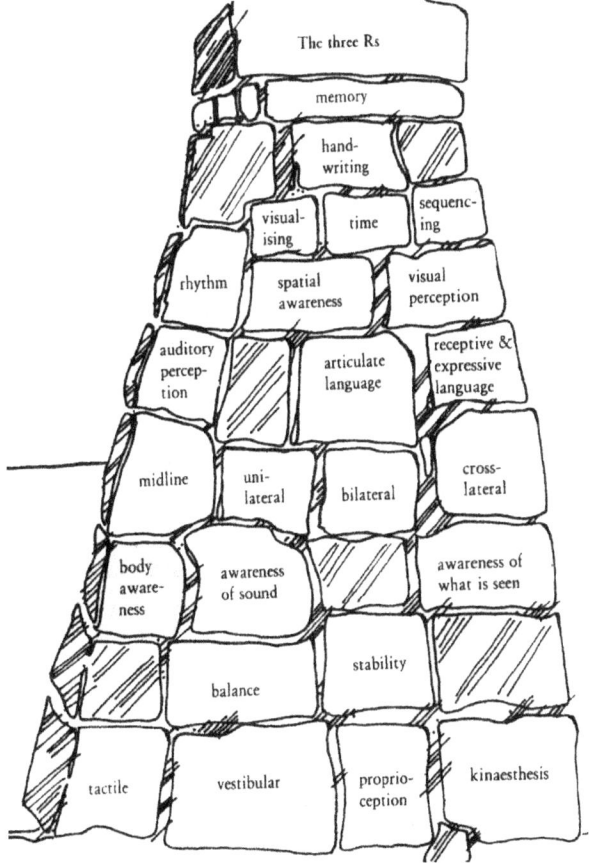

The pyramid of learning. (Illustration used with permission)

need to establish a firm foundation and build on it. Through exploration and movement, the two sides of the brain interact. When the brain has integrated, then children are ready for formal learning. Introducing children to abstract concepts before they are ready is actually counterproductive. 'To attempt formal learning before integration takes place, either before or after seven years of age, will usually result in frustration, struggle and often defeat.'[17] It is interesting to note that children begin school in Scandinavian countries at seven years of age, and they tend to have the most successful outcomes.

So while exposure to 'formal academic' learning before the building blocks have been established only leads to frustration and failure; early exposure to a stimulating, 'informal and natural' learning environment is very beneficial.

Interestingly, in his popular book *Raising Boys*, Steve Biddulph identifies the characteristic that young boys often mature at a slower rate than girls, and suggests that if they began formal schooling a little older, they might experience more success.[19]

The different learning styles

Not all children learn in the same way. Generally, very young children are kinaesthetic learners. They need hands-on activities using concrete materials in order to learn. Most teachers tend to be visual learners and they often use visual learning tools to teach their students. This might involve lots of whiteboard activity, book work and the use of other printed material. However, some children are predominantly auditory learners. These are often the ones who appear to be not paying attention at group time, but have in fact processed what has been said.

Howard Gardner described a way of looking at different mindsets and talents with his approach to multiple intelligences. Through his work, he explained that different learners have a preference in ways of expressing their understanding and talents. Gardner classified verbal/linguistic learners, visual/spatial learners, musical, logical mathematical, interpersonal, naturalistic, body/kinaesthetic, and intrapersonal approaches to learning. To provide an authentic education, our education system needs to recognise and cater for different learning styles.

The brain and plasticity

While scientists continue to examine and research the brain, educational professionals are noting the relevance of this research and how it relates to learning.

In *Mindsight*, Dan Siegel's discussion of brain function highlights the necessity of integration of the two halves of the brain for fully functioning development. Non-verbal signals are created and perceived by the right hemisphere, which is dominant during the first years of life. Babies use non-verbal communication, such as facial expression, voice tone and gestures to inform their caregivers of their needs. 'We know that the left hemisphere is coming online when two and three-year-old children start asking, Why? Why? Why?'[20]

As a thumbnail sketch of each mode, he has described the qualities of the left side of the brain as 'later developing, linear, linguistic, logical, literal, labels, lists', and the right as 'early developing, holistic, non-verbal, images, metaphors, whole body sense, raw emotion, stress reduction and autobiographical memory'.[21] This demonstrates the relevance and significance of readiness for abstract, academic learning.

Interestingly, Siegel notes that the early immaturity (the lack of connections between the different regions of the brain) 'is what gives us that openness of experience that is so crucial to learning'.[22] This is an advantage to young children, who are not hampered by preconceived ideas.

Under the right conditions, neural firing can lead to the strengthening of synaptic connections. These conditions include 'repetition, emotional arousal, novelty and the careful focus of attention'[23] and they are vital to learning in the classroom. The brain actually changes physically in response to new experiences, and this plasticity applies throughout life.

The plasticity of the brain was also eloquently demonstrated by Jill Bolt Taylor PhD, a brain scientist who suffered a stroke and had to learn how to regain her balance and walk, and relearn how to read. During her recovery, she recorded observations of her own mind. She described how the euphoric peace of the intuitive right brain (existing in the present moment) became more dominant as the left brain, which catered for logical awareness, was damaged. Her experience demonstrates the difficulties of children with learning disabilities. In her book *My Stroke of Insight*, Taylor described how she saw the abstract representation of squiggles on the page, and she came to realise these squiggles had names and sounds and that their combinations had meaning attached.

Learning difficulties

Children identified with learning difficulties often have neurological immaturities. The processing system in the brain requires sequential learning and the brain receives its stimulus from the eyes, the ears, the skin and the muscles. As already noted, integration of the two halves of the brain is required for successful learning. Babies' brains are wired with primitive reflexes. These are automatic motor activities that do not require planning. A newborn will grip an adult's finger tightly and often appear to have jerky movements. The child who grips his pencil so tightly that written work becomes tiring is likely to have retained these reflexes after they are not needed or useful.

Dyspraxia is defined by the dictionary as 'a neurological disorder in which messages from the brain to the muscles are disrupted' and this may affect different functions such as speaking, eating, writing, reading and activities requiring coordination of the limbs such as running and skipping. Children with dyspraxia have difficulty planning and executing different functions such as speech and coordination. If their tactile, vestibular, proprioceptive and kinaesthetic systems are immature, their brains may not be fully integrated, and they are likely to experience problems with auditory and visual processing. These skills are basic to reading and writing ability.

As mentioned earlier in the discussion on learning through the senses; hearing is the passive reception of sound. Listening involves the brain function of processing the information you've heard and interpreting it. If there is a delay or an interruption, then learning difficulties often follow and children can experience problems with language development. The inability to focus, process information correctly, concentrate and remember invariably leads to poor vocabulary, speech and comprehension.

In the same way, vision is not simply a matter of being able to see. Fast and efficient neural connections are necessary for children to interpret and understand what they see. They need to be able to use both eyes together efficiently. They need to track moving objects, be able to focus, and develop depth perception and peripheral vision.

If you could imagine seeing the page through the eyes of a child with visual processing problems, the words and letters might not necessarily lie in a straight line. They might appear to be all over the place, and might not be grouped together. They might merge in an arbitrary fashion. For example, Iw as at th e s hop s. Children who have trouble reading have difficulty because they can't look ahead, they lose their place, they skip words and they cannot concentrate. These children spend a lot more energy processing simple tasks because they encounter major difficulties and they often feel exhausted, uninspired and defeated.

Barbara Arrowsmith Young, herself disabled from childhood, developed exercises to help learning-disabled children. She noted 'These children are often accused of being careless but actually their overloaded brains fire the wrong motor movements.'[24]

Gerry Kennedy, an independent consultant in inclusive technology, believes too many highly intelligent children were being written off by society because they had difficulty reading and writing. 'Our education system is based on the premise of learning information and regurgitating it in exam-type conditions.' He added, 'Traditional assessments don't work for kids who are not confident with text in the way most educators deem success to be rated.'[25]

So what causes learning delays? They can be caused by a variety of factors and circumstances. Heredity can play a part, as can the environment in which a child is raised. Early-childhood illnesses such as repeated ear infections can significantly affect auditory processing ability. Allergies to various foods, and sensitivities to chemicals, additives and preservatives in processed food, and environmental-pollutants can all impact on a child's ability to learn.

> 'Teach your students to use what talents they have; the woods would be silent if no bird sang except those that sing best.'
> – Anonymous

Summary

For learning to be successful, it has to be relevant and meaningful. It needs to be considered a process rather than a body of knowledge. It needs to be comprehensive and it is most effective when delivered in a supportive and stimulating environment. Constant testing of a narrow range of core subjects definitely does not satisfy the requirements for authentic learning. Instead it promotes rote learning, memorising and regurgitating facts. It curbs creativity and divergent thinking and leads to boredom and disengagement. Studying with the narrow focus of passing a test is never lasting or even useful because information without meaning is not understood and is quickly forgotten, as the old Chinese proverb elaborates:

> Tell me and I'll forget
> Show me and I may remember
> Involve me and I'll understand.

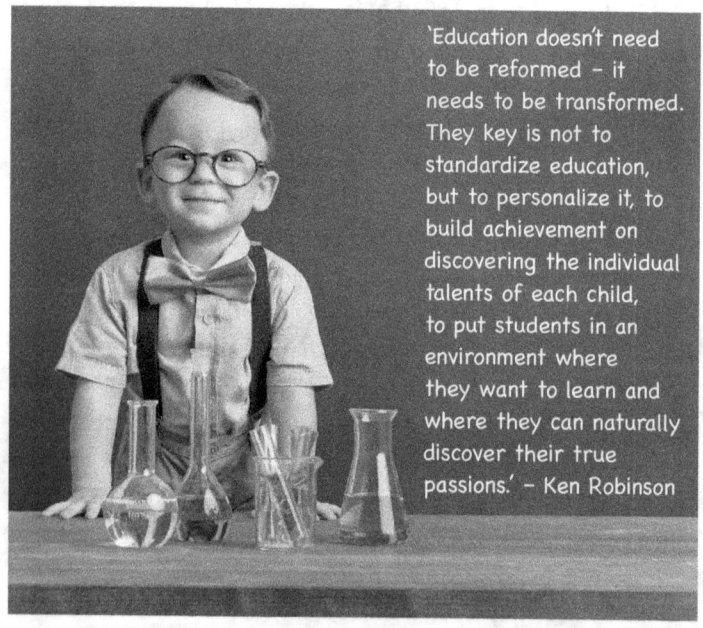

'Education doesn't need to be reformed – it needs to be transformed. They key is not to standardize education, but to personalize it, to build achievement on discovering the individual talents of each child, to put students in an environment where they want to learn and where they can naturally discover their true passions.' – Ken Robinson

3

The Role of the Teacher

> 'The aim of education should be to teach the child to think, not what to think.' – John Dewey

The teacher's role is to facilitate learning. Instruction is one element of the role but it is not the sole or even major component of teaching. Kathy Walker is an Australian early childhood expert on play-based learning. She established the Walker Learning Approach, which includes explicit instruction but advocates a child-centred, holistic approach.[1] Learning is not simply a system of transferring knowledge from one person to another, as if filling an empty vessel with information. Passive learning often occurs when studying for a test. Without the elements of relevance and active engagement, it is meaningless. It is far more useful to train students with skills that equip them to become independent thinkers, to be able to search for relevant information, to prioritise and to critically analyse and assess its suitability for the task. Successful teachers encourage children to question and reflect, and even to adopt the mindset 'Is there something I don't know that I should know?'

The teacher's purpose is to help students achieve their personal best and reach their potential. Recognising the element of effort is a great motivator. By understanding the principles of how children learn, and by providing motivation, encouragement and support, by providing positive feedback and constructive criticism, by questioning and challenging, and by making learning enjoyable, teachers can maximise their students' potential for success.

When planning an education program, teachers first establish an ideal learning environment. They observe and assess their students' abilities. After establishing needs and strengths, they develop a suitable program based on a firm foundation. Teachers constantly monitor their students' progress to determine the relevance and effectiveness of their teaching and regularly inform parents of their children's progress.

> 'Sometimes our light goes out but is blown into flame by another human being. Each of us owes deepest thanks to those who have rekindled this light.' – Albert Schweitzer

Establishing a positive learning environment

Classroom teachers have to first establish a relationship of mutual trust and respect with their students. They determine clear expectations and create a positive learning environment by taking into consideration the needs of all of their students.

Teachers are alert to environmental factors that could interfere with learning. They design an environment which encompasses the delicate balance of enthusiasm and stimulation, while also catering for the stability of a secure, calm atmosphere. This is especially relevant if the class includes autistic children or children with learning difficulties or behavioural problems. Some children, for instance, are particularly sensitive to fluorescent lighting, while others find that black print on stark white paper is difficult to look at. Others cannot tolerate high noise levels. Some benefit from slope boards, much like the old-fashioned desks, which allow and encourage correct posture for reading and writing. The recommended angle for slope boards is twenty degrees. This enables the head to be held at the optimal angle, with the neck in a comfortable position, not bent too far over, creating a more natural angle for the eyes to meet the page.

Recognising the vital role of nutrition in learning, many schools now cater for a fruit break and ensure students have access to water to maintain adequate hydration.

Effective programs cater for the physical needs of students as well. Timetabling active breaks during sessions maintains interest and engagement. Gareth Malone, a British choirmaster, recognised this need and used his skills to re-engage boys who were not succeeding academically. In 2010, Gareth joined the staff at Peer Tree Mead

Primary School in Essex. He introduced his pupils to the concept of 'unbridled competition, risk and adventure'. He relocated drama classes to the forest, where the boys were required to prepare and read scripts. They designed and choreographed a concert for their parents and in the process gained not only in self-esteem but also in improved literacy skills. Gareth's mission was 'to harness the power of boisterous behaviour and challenge the boys' apparent aversion to standing out from the crowd so that they would feel more confident about aiming for better grades'.

In recent years, we have seen the growth of forest kindergartens in Germany, Denmark, the UK, USA and Canada. This style of preschool education caters for three to six-year-olds and is conducted almost exclusively outdoors. Children are encouraged to play, explore and learn in the forest or similar natural environment. The role of adult supervisors is to assist rather than lead, and children create their own play fashioned out of objects found in nature, rather than manufactured toys that come with a predefined meaning or purpose. This has created a stimulating education whereby children develop skills through using their imagination, engaging in role play, and building creative constructions. Children involved in forest kindergartens have been found to have increased balance and agility, coordination, depth perception, risk assessment skills and a healthy resilience. 'When children from German Waldkindergartens go to primary school teachers observe a significant improvement in reading, writing, mathematics, social interactions and many other areas.'[2] This movement has gained in popularity as a reaction to the academic push in early years, accompanied by standardised testing that has dominated the education systems of many developed nations.

> 'We cannot teach people anything; we can only help them discover it within themselves.' – Galileo Galilei

Assessing students' needs

When children enter school, they come with a set of skills already established. Teachers ascertain their stage of development and design appropriate programs to cater for their needs. While assessing ability levels, the trained eye of the teacher is looking for skills and potential problems such as

- level of concentration
- possible vision and hearing problems
- speech delays and limited vocabulary
- the ability to follow directions
- the ability to complete tasks
- the ability to organise themselves
- level of impulsivity
- letter reversals (although these are common among young children)
- difficulties with coordination and balance
- poor muscle tone
- poor proprioception (body awareness and position in space).

Comprehensive screening programs such as Dr Pye Twaddell's Early Kindergarten Screening Assessment[3] alert teachers to potential problems which can be addressed before children experience and identify with failure.

Hearing and vision problems are the most obvious to identify and they can profoundly interfere with learning. Sight tests alone will not reveal the extent of vision problems. If children are examined by a behavioural optometrist, they will undergo detailed assessment which monitors whether the eyes are tracking together and whether they can refocus from a distance to close-up. Specialists are trained to look for signs such as whether the eyes are rolling, whether there is excessive blinking, if children are tilting their heads and rubbing their eyes, whether they frequently lose their place when reading and whether they are producing letter reversals, or mirror imaging. The skill of reading requires rapid, successive saccadic eye movements and this development does not fully mature until about the age of eight years. The late highly respected behavioural optometrist Sue Larter questioned why we are trying to teach five-year-olds to read. She noted that in places such as Korea, where children enter formal education at an early age, many require glasses by the middle childhood years.

When children are constantly distracted and not paying attention in class, it is often due to hearing and auditory processing problems. Auditory processing requires fast and efficient neural connections as well as the ability to identify and make sense of what you are hearing. If children have a history of ear infections in early childhood, their listening skills may have been compromised at a vital stage of development. If children cannot distinguish between similar sounds spoken quickly, they don't hear accurately and therefore cannot reproduce accurately. These children have to exert a lot of effort in decoding words. When teachers observe speech and language disorders in them, the obvious course of action is to have their auditory perception tested.

Most developmental delays are linked and there is never one simple answer to addressing a learning problem. Teachers in early childhood classes are trained to observe and assess students in a holistic fashion. If children present with coordination problems, teachers will analyse the state of their vestibular and proprioceptive systems. If a child experiences difficulties with any of these systems, they are less likely to understand and master abstract representations on paper. Quite obviously, these problems need to be overcome before we can start scaffolding formal learning.

Associated professionals

It is helpful for teachers to be aware of other professionals and specialised programs available outside the classroom so that they can incorporate them into the classroom program or alert parents and advise them of potentially helpful referrals. Many specialised professionals offer skills and tools to assist with targeted problems. I first became aware of the expertise of associated professions when I was given the responsibility of teaching the first Early Intervention Unit in Belconnen, Canberra, in the 1990s. To assist children with special needs, I worked with a team of experts from the Child Health and Development Service (CHADS). The group consisted of a speech therapist, a physiotherapist, an occupational therapist and a social worker. The team assisted each child at various stages and we regularly consulted to assess and evaluate individual needs.

As a teacher, I learnt so much from this wide field of experts.

Until then, I was unaware of the detailed analysis involved when an occupational therapist assesses a child's coordination problems with handwriting. Occupational therapists (OTs) have intrinsic knowledge of specific sequential stages of pencil grip. Children progress from the fisted or palmar grip before they are able to adopt the functional, mature three-fingered pencil grip or dynamic tripod posture. OTs have alerted us to the significance of muscle tone, upper body strength and stability, and a natural seating posture. They have devised programs with gross motor exercises that strengthen the shoulder girdle and core muscles; and specific exercises such as finger-wrestling and playing with pegs, that are also designed to strengthen and improve fine motor control and coordination.

Educational kinesiologists offer associated expertise to help overcome learning difficulties. To assist with proprioception and vestibular difficulties, therapy might include playing with weights, bouncing on a trampoline, exercises that cross the mid-line, whole-body exercises such as crab crawling, visual tracking of lazy eights, practising on balance boards, skipping exercises and crawling games, hanging upside down, rocking, spinning, rolling and dancing.

I have personally witnessed dramatic improvements in children with special needs after chiropractic treatment. I saw a little boy who could hardly grasp a pencil making random marks on a page, and when he returned from a session with the chiropractor he was able to draw a recognisable stick figure of 'Daddy'.

Speech therapists as well have a deep appreciation for the significance of the problems associated with visual and auditory processing and how these skills affect speech development. Their specific therapy often includes listening games and visual differentiation activities.

Doctors also play a role in determining and identifying possible inhibitors to learning. Teachers are aware that allergies and food sensitivities, and chemical intolerances can severely impact a child's learning ability. Dr Marilyn Dyson is an expert in identifying problems associated with nutrition and biochemistry.[4] She is concerned about the poor diet of many young Australians and recommends that children with delays should be assessed for nutritional imbalance. When children present with dark rings around their eyes, pale and pasty complexions, puffiness, low muscle tone, red ears or cheeks, allergies are an obvious suspect and these children could have compromised immune systems.

Common toxins that can interfere with a child's learning can be found in insecticides and pesticides, prescription drugs, trans fats, soft drinks, perfumes and cosmetics, industrial cleaning products, processed meats, high-fructose corn syrup, chlorinated water, toxic fish and heavy metals such as mercury or lead. Lead is a naturally occurring heavy metal, often used in industry, and it can be toxic when ingested or inhaled. Children are particularly sensitive and susceptible to the effects of lead 'as they absorb more lead into their bloodstream and retain more lead in their bodies',[5] and because 'their brains are still at the developing stage'.[6] 'Lead exposure in childhood can cause behaviour and attention problems, learning difficulties and cognitive losses.' Parents can limit exposure by avoiding contact with house renovations built before 1970, avoiding lead paint in imported toys and distancing exposure to mining and smelting occupations as well as various hobbies such as glazed pottery and stained glass.

Specialist educational programs

In addition to the option of referral to specialist therapies, teachers also have access to many programs designed to enhance learning development. Move to Learn, Brain Gym, the Listening Program, Sensory Integration Therapy and Sound Therapy are all very useful programs that have proven to assist learning.

Move To Learn was developed by Barbara Pheloung over thirty years ago.[7] The program conducted research through the University of Sydney, and is based on the principle that movement is fundamental for learning. It involves a series of specifically designed exercises and practised movements that assist with integrating the two hemispheres of the brain. Pheloung wrote several books on learning difficulties and prepared an online checklist for parents who wish to identify and eliminate particular problems associated with their child's learning. To access the free interactive LD profile test, visit the More To Learn website (www.movetolearn.com.au).

Brain Gym is another effective movement-based program of simple, integrated cross-lateral movements designed to assist learning. When our son was little, he suffered from sinus congestion. He was aware I had been using Brain Gym with my students and asked if he could learn it. After a couple of months, I received a phone call from his teacher. She wanted to know what I'd been doing with him as his concentration had improved noticeably. When Brain Gym is incorporated into the morning routine, children begin the day ready to learn.[8] Carla Hannaford elaborates on Brain Gym in her book *Smart Moves*.

The Listening Program is 'a music-based auditory stimulation method that is used to train the auditory skills needed to effectively listen, learn and communicate. It consists of an extensive series of high quality audio CDs that integrate specially produced acoustic music, primarily classical with innovative sound processing techniques'.[9] The method is based on key concepts of Sound Therapy, which originated with Alfred Tomatis MD. Tomatis was a French ear, nose and throat specialist in the 1940s. His program involves music, voice and nature sounds that were specifically filtered to enhance particular sounds to stimulate the brain's processing regions. His work was further developed by Ingo Steinbeck, a German sound engineer, who created the high-frequency Samonas Sound Therapy CDs.

Barbara Arrowsmith-Young is another pioneer in brain plasticity and learning. As a child she suffered from learning disabilities and had to exert extra effort just to keep up. As an adult she realised the cause of her problem and developed targeted brain exercises such as tracing complex lines or rote memorising. These specific exercises strengthen the weakened brain function. Children who appear socially clumsy and are unable to interpret non-verbal cues, or are impulsive or disorganised and have difficulty with planning and setting goals, often have frontal lobe deficits. What they need is a rich, stimulating environment that encourages brain development. This is far more productive than tutoring and repeating lessons they cannot comprehend. Norm Doidge commented, 'Barbara Arrowsmith Young's work compels us to imagine how much good might be accomplished if every child had a brain-based assessment, and if problems were found, a tailor made program created to strengthen essential areas in the early years, when neuroplasticity is greatest.'[10] In the USA, the recently announced Brain

Initiative, a program of research into neuroscience and nanoscience, demonstrates an awareness of the significance of understanding how the brain works and how we learn. Hopefully, this initiative will lead to essential support in this field.[11]

Fast ForWord is another training program achieving impressive results for children with language impairments and related learning difficulties. It was designed with the help of Michael Merzenich, one of the world's leading researchers in brain plasticity. His Scientific Learning staff includes 'child psychologists, plasticity researchers, engineers, programmers and animators'.[12] The team has devised a computer program that captivates the child's attention and continually rewards each achievement. The child is given de-coding and comprehension exercises and the results are impressive. 'The average child who took the program moved ahead 1.8 years of language development in six weeks.'[13]

Posit Science is a related program designed to extend mental lifespan by challenging adults as they age. I have practised the visual and auditory programs and found them stimulating, if not frustrating at times. This is because the more you succeed, the harder the tasks become, which is exactly the point. These mental exercises increase your ability to concentrate and remain mentally alert. 'To keep the mind active requires learning something truly new with intense focus.'[14]

There are many related professionals and specialised programs that are available to enhance learning in the classroom and teachers regularly upgrade their professional learning to ensure that their students benefit from the best opportunities available. This quote from Ignacio Estrada illustrates the significance of effective teaching in today's classrooms: 'If a child can't learn the way we teach, may be we should teach the way they learn.'

Developing an educational program

> 'In teaching it is the method and not the content that is the message…the drawing out, not the pumping in.' – Ashley Montagu

Having thoroughly assessed their students' needs, teachers are then in the best position to design the most relevant program. In today's classrooms, teachers are often required to develop an independent learning plan (ILP) for individual children. This requires extensive knowledge of each student's progress and it must be monitored as needs change. Beginning with a firm foundation, teachers are then able to scaffold learning and challenge students to achieve their potential.

Providing a rich and varied program that caters for different learning styles requires extensive planning and preparation. In the early years, it is particularly important to create lessons that are relevant and meaningful. To demonstrate on a practical level, I can relate several lessons typical of an early childhood classroom.

When giving a practical lesson on the study of capacity, for example, children might experiment with a variety of vessels and water. The skills of prediction and estimation are reinforced with each experiment. To demonstrate the relevance of the lesson, the teacher might relate it to an everyday experience at home. When Mum opens a large tin of peaches and shares it out for dessert, she needs to estimate how much to distribute so there is enough for everybody; and if there is some left, she would need to find a container that would, by her estimate, be the right size for the contents.

For an everyday example of learning with numbers, children can observe that Mum and Dad need to estimate how many groceries they will need for the week, and how much the trolley load will cost.

Being aware of the relevance of what they're learning, students are more likely to be interested and engaged. Incorporating and utilising wonderful resources such as stories often enhances the understanding of a concept. In *Mr Archimedes' Bath*, by Pamela Allen, Mr Archimedes blames his animal friends for the changing level of the bath water each time one gets out or back in. Finally he realises that displacement is responsible for the phenomenon. By asking questions, a teacher can determine whether the student is confusing weight with mass. One little boy's explanation went, 'Well, it's like if there was a whole lot of boxes in the bath, and you get in…they would be moved over.'

In Pat Hutchins's story *The Doorbell Rang*, she explores the concept of sharing, or division. Ma makes a batch of cookies, and each time visitors arrive, the cookies have to be shared between more people, the result being fewer cookies for each child. To engage the children,

I have prepared a kit with laminated photos of cookies, plastic plates, and a battery-powered doorbell buzzer. I invite the children to act out the story, but first we predict what will happen and how many cookies are left each time they have to be redistributed. So while they are having fun, they are incorporating mathematical concepts and it's an experience they will remember. However, it can backfire. One time a little boy with autism actually began chewing on the laminated cookies. I reasoned that at least he was actively engaged. He had been watching from a distance and was drawn into the activity.

Such a lesson can be extended by having a cooking session with all the learning possibilities of estimating and predicting, measuring and observing the properties of dry and liquid matter and the effect of heat on dough.

To enhance mathematical concepts, young children benefit most from practical, hands-on games. Given a set of small wooden cut-outs and felt teaching aids, they can engage in games designed to make learning fun. Given the directions, 'Share 9 fish between 3 bowls' they should first estimate how many fish go in each bowl; then test their prediction. Other simple games could involve placing 10 butterflies evenly on 5 flowers; 8 boats on 2 lakes; or 12 snails on 4 leaves. By questioning their reasoning, the teacher is able to understand the strategies used, the thinking process and the level of comprehension of these mathematical concepts.

Real experiences with personal involvement always lead to more comprehensive understanding of concepts. To gain a realistic concept of the size of something very large such as a brontosaurus, stating the measurement alone would be meaningless. If you direct the class to lie down end-to-end up the hallway, count and take measurements and photos, the discussion afterwards would reveal not only engagement in learning but also the associated excitement of an experience they would remember.

With young children, it is never difficult to stimulate an interest in nature and science. Their interest in such concepts comes naturally. When you think about it, the world is a relatively new experience to them, and I never cease to be amazed and refreshed by their wonderment and fascination and their eagerness to experiment.

Endeavouring to inspire creative writing is sometimes challenging, particularly if the student thinks she can't do it. Encouraging a child to have a go is the starting point. One little girl in my kindergarten class was struggling to think of a topic. Her big brother had had an extended period of hospitalisation and Christmas was nearing. When I reminded her of what was going to happen in her family shortly, her eyes lit up and creativity flowed. She wrotre the following piece, 'Ross is coming home'.

Being aware of your student's interests and experiences assists with planning appropriate and relevant programs. Encouraging students to take measured risks and to accept that we learn from our mistakes is another valuable lesson.

> 'Children are uncut jewels with invaluable potential. Teachers are jewellers with tools for making futures priceless.'
> – Angela Harper Brooks

Assessing educational programs

Teachers continually monitor their students' progress using a variety of methods and tools. These include observations, anecdotal records, checklists, running records of reading ability, regular pre- and post-testing and collecting samples of work for portfolios. All assessments are moderated between teachers of comparable classes to overcome subjectivity and ensure fairness. Teachers regularly inform parents via parent–teacher interviews, learning journeys to showcase work and formal reporting, as well compiling and providing up to date portfolios of their child's work along with updated checklists of continuous assessment.

When testing children, we are not necessarily looking for a single, correct answer. We are checking their thought processes and analysing how they arrived at a particular answer. Given pictures or words of matching objects, most children might pair a brush with a comb. But the child who pairs a brush with a dog is approaching the task in a different manner and is probably more likely to be a divergent thinker. Most sequencing cards show objects going from smaller to larger. A seed grows into a plant, a baby to an adult. However, when a child is given a series of cards showing a candle melting, the one who realises that the sequence is in reverse indicates he is really thinking about the task.

> 'The teacher asked, "Tell me, Johnny, if I had nine apples and there were twelve children, how would I divide them equally?" Johnny thought for a moment then replied happily, "Make apple sauce."' –
> Helen Rudin

A typical kindergarten literacy and numeracy checklist might include details of whether a student is operating at the emergent or extended stages of reading, viewing, speaking and listening, and writing. Progressive checklists include detailed analysis of each area. To take writing as an example, teachers are looking for whether the child writes his own name, and is able to write a small bank of personal words; attempts familiar forms of writing (lists, letters. recounts, stories); attempts to use some features of written language such as capital letters and full stops; recognises that writing has a specific purpose to communicate meaning to others, writes spontaneously for self rather than for an audience; and whether content of writing can be understood by others.

Checklists for mathematical skills encompass the child's ability to understand number, measurement, chance and data and the degree of his ability to work mathematically. When considering number, teachers are looking for whether the child can count, write, compare and order numbers 1 to 10 and 10 to 20; match collections by number and symbol; whether she can combine concrete materials to informally add; whether she has achieved one-to-one correspondence; can explore subtraction by separating and comparing collections; copy and continue number patterns; count by 1s, 2s, 10s; count orally to 10 or 20 forwards and backwards ; understand ordinal numbers (and the concepts of before/after, bigger/smaller).

An example of a mathematical test commonly used in the early years is SENA testing from the Count Me In Too program. Here teachers individually test students to evaluate their ability with numeral identification, forward and backward number word sequence, subitising and early arithmetic strategies. Using counters, students demonstrate their level of comprehension of the concepts addition and subtraction, multiplication and division. One activity involves giving more than twelve counters randomly spaced, and the student is instructed to make three groups of four in each group, and asked how many are there all together. By observing and asking questions, teachers are able to understand the strategies used by a student. By rearranging the same number of counters so the groups appear different, teachers can see whether the child has mastered the concept of constancy. This can also be tested by changing the shape of a ball of play dough and asking questions about whether the child thinks there is more, less or the same amount. I remember one little boy who had obviously not mastered the skills of grouping and counting on from the largest number. He needed to count on to twelve, and after using all his fingers he paused for a minute, then politely asked, 'May I please borrow two fingers?'

Formal reports clearly demonstrate the detail and depth of understanding required of each child's development. Indicating the level of reading and writing ability, a teacher might typically describe a child's progress in the following manner. 'She reads for meaning, uses expression and employs predictive strategies. She self-corrects and expresses text confidently and fluently. She has a good knowledge of word formation and creates stories independently. Her handwriting is sometimes a little rushed and she is concentrating on keeping the letters a consistent size.'

Teachers in early childhood classes use running records to monitor reading progress. This individual assessment involves listening to a child reading, counting the number of correct words in the text, and using a formula to determine progress. Teachers are able to analyse decoding skills by listening and checking for whether the child is sounding out individual letters or grouping letter combinations, looking ahead and using appropriate expression. Comprehension is then tested to determine the level of understanding of the text.

What I have described occurs in early childhood classes. Throughout their schooling, students are continually assessed to determine progress. The intensive level of assessment required demonstrates that parents today are extremely well informed of their child's development. Politicians reveal their ignorance of the facts when they assume or suggest that parents are not informed of their child's schooling and that they 'deserve to know'.

Despite what some sections of the media would have you believe, the level of a child's success at school is not solely determined by his teacher. Many related factors directly affect a child's development. Socio-economic background and the degree of support from home both have an enormous influence on how well a child succeeds. Whether there are learning difficulties or English as a Second Language issues, many other related factors influence and to some extent determine future success. Using their training and skills teachers maximise every opportunity to help students reach their potential.

However, despite their dedication and commitment, teachers in today's western societies, including Australia, UK and USA often feel vilified by politicians, members of the public, and by the tabloid press. It's time our society recognised the worth of teachers and appreciated their contribution to the next generation.

4

Valuing Teachers

> 'A teacher affects eternity: he can never tell where his influence stops.' – Henry Adams

Most of us remember at least one favourite teacher, someone who inspired us, someone who recognised a talent and fostered a belief in ourselves, someone who made a difference. Of course we also regarded some others with rather less affection, or even disdain. Such is the nature of any profession with its full range of personalities, talents and abilities.

My favourite teacher was Miss Carey from Year 5/6. When I tried to analyse why in particular she stood out above the rest, it came down to the fact that she treated us with respect. She made school inviting by providing interesting, relevant and engaging activities. We felt secure and happy to be there.

Izzeldin Abuelaish, a successful Palestinian doctor who grew up in poverty in Gaza, saw education as his salvation.[1] While his parents needed to put all their efforts into survival for the family, it was his teachers who gave him hope for the future. He was grateful for the opportunity to go to school, and he was especially grateful to one special teacher. 'By the end of the year he had convinced me, a first grader, that I could learn anything I wanted to learn and become anything I wanted to become. He was an extraordinary man.' Despite his desperate situation, Izzeldin appreciated the opportunities that came his way. 'I was lucky that so many of my teachers reached out to help me. They are the ones who boosted my energy and gave me the self-confidence to carry on. It was the teachers rather than my parents who opened doors for me and let me know there was a future apart from the grinding poverty, in which I lived.'[2]

There are many more examples of exemplary teachers who have been credited with playing a pivotal role in the success of notable people. But here in Australia, in recent years the role of the teacher has been undermined and attacked by politicians, the media and many others in our society.

> 'There is no more noble profession than teaching. A great teacher is a great artist, but his medium is not canvas but the human soul.'
> – Anonymous

Criticisms, myths and misconceptions

Parents, politicians and adults in general feel entitled to judge the school system and its teachers because they feel some degree of familiarity with it. After all, we all have had the shared experience of attending school, even if it was many years ago, and that qualifies us as experts!

Conservative members of the population sometimes look nostalgically at 'the good old days' when everything was right with the world. When students learnt their ABCs and everybody learnt how to spell properly. But when you examine the situation, the facts don't support such assumptions. 'Australians are more educated today than they have been at any other point in history.' Right now more than half the population (51%) aged 15 to 64 has a post-secondary qualification.[3]

A generation or two ago, conditions were different. Teacher training was a two-year course. Class sizes were anything from 40 to 60. However, expectations were also different. Children sat in rows according to ability. Those in the dumb row certainly knew about it. It was seared into their identity and they spent their lives with a limited belief in themselves and their ability. Children were lectured to and reporting to parents was minimal. Teachers taught the same subject matter to the whole class regardless of students' abilities or learning styles, and discipline was maintained using spurious methods such as corporal punishment. I fail to see how fear could ever be an incentive for improvement, particularly if the students subjected to it were experiencing genuine learning difficulties. My dad told the story of a group of boys regularly lining up to get 'the cuts' across their knuckles because they didn't know their times tables. How could that ever serve to encourage understanding and a love of learning? My mum also recalled the headmaster of her school walking up the aisle between the desks indiscriminately flicking his cane at whoever happened to be in the way. On the other hand, she also reminisced about some wonderful teachers who she could clearly remember and she would often quote their inspirational sayings many years later.

The headlines would have you believe that schoolyard bullying has become a major issue. But they ignore the fact that bullying has always played a part in society. Schools today take bullying very seriously. Students are explicitly taught to not tolerate bullying, to not engage in onlooker activity and to report bullying. They are reassured that they can expect follow up and consequences via conferencing and counselling for both the victim and the perpetrator. Admittedly, cyber bullying has made effective action more difficult, particularly as much of it takes place anytime, anywhere, not just in the schoolyard.

At one stage, I was naive enough to associate bullying exclusively with schooldays, but of course people who bully often grow up to become bullies in the workplace, especially if their problem wasn't addressed or resolved in their youth.

In Finland, schools use a very effective anti-bullying program, Ki Va. The program encourages each individual to share and assume responsible for the school's anti-bullying culture, which encompasses verbal, physical and cyber bullying. The resulting reduced level of anxiety has been credited with contributing to increased academic performance.

We are often told crime is escalating; but again, the statistics indicate otherwise. The Australian Institute of Criminology recently released a report 'which shows that Australia's homicide rate remains at historic lows'. The difference is the twenty-four hour news cycle. It's visual. It's graphic and it's repeated for dramatic effect. It has created a very anxious, insecure society. Similarly, vandalism is reported as out of control. Our grandfathers used to blow up letter boxes with crackers, but that was 'just a bit of fun', wasn't it?

Media also report a decline in discipline in schools, particularly government schools. 'Government schools teach the majority of students from poor families, the majority of students with disability, and the majority of indigenous and migrant students.'[4] These are the communities with greatest need. When children with behavioural problems, or other factors that impede learning, have outworn their welcome in private and independent schools, government schools have no choice but to accept them and endeavour to help with whatever resources they have available.

Of course those students of previous generations who were caned never repeated their misdemeanours, did they? If getting the cuts was so effective as a discipline tool, why then were the same students back for more, time and time again?

Teachers will never be given the respect and authority for effective discipline while some politicians and media refer to them in disparaging terms and some parents discuss perceived grievances in front of their children.

> 'If you can read this, thank a teacher.' – Bumper sticker

Cartoonists have an uncanny ability to gauge and succinctly represent community perceptions and concerns. French cartoonist Emmanual Chaunu created a now famous cartoon that poignantly reflects the changing attitudes of society towards teachers and education. He uses two contrasting scenarios. The first scene, from 1969, portrays a teacher and two parents berating a child for poor marks, with the comment, 'What's wrong with those grades?' The second scene, from 2009, shows the parents berating the teacher with the same comment while the student expresses smug satisfaction.

In recent years, select politicians and certain sections of the media have coined the term 'under-performing teachers'. Their constant and repeated reference implies we are in the midst of a crisis with an epidemic of inadequately-trained teaching staff. In many countries, particularly in Scandinavia and Asia, the teaching profession is highly respected. In Australia, teachers have become convenient scapegoats to deflect attention from policy issues and to fill in gaps in the media cycle. A favoured method is to repeat something often enough so that eventually people will begin to believe it and accept it as factual. Their claims are unsubstantiated. The fact that Australian students perform as well as they do is largely due to the skills and dedication of their teachers despite the lack of investment in education over the previous decade. These attacks are demeaning and they undermine public respect for the teaching profession.

During the debate regarding teacher quality and university entrance standards for selection of candidates, reference has even been made to 'toxic teachers'.[5] Such negative, emotive language is detrimental to the debate. The Australian Catholic University Vice-Chancellor, Greg Craven, has warned that narrowly focusing on Australian Tertiary Admission Rank (ATAR) scores would not necessarily produce superior quality teachers.[6] Choosing suitable candidates is not as simplistic as that. He stated that ATAR scores were skewed against people from lower socio-economic backgrounds and failed to predict success at university. 'What really matters is the quality of a student once they have completed their university degree, not when they enter.'

I spent several years working with teaching interns from the University of Canberra. Standards were taken very seriously and course and practical work was thoroughly evaluated. If the academic standard or any other relevant criteria were not acceptable, the interns did not graduate. As a classroom teacher while preparing reports on pre-service teachers, the ultimate consideration was 'Would you be prepared to work with this person as a teaching partner; and would you have confidence in his or her ability to teach your own children?'

There are many complexities involved in addressing the criteria for suitable candidates for teaching. We do need high-calibre applicants but, as the medical profession has acknowledged, academic success is not the only measure, nor does it guarantee an effective professional. Prospective teachers should perhaps be assessed using a variety of measurements such as personality profiles and level of social and emotional intelligence. The type of person who makes a good teacher should be highly motivated and committed, and be able to demonstrate well-developed interpersonal and relationship skills. Tests and scales have been created to assess social intelligence. The Profile of

Non Verbal Sensitivity (PONS) uses photos, video snippets and voices, to evaluate people's responses and assess their interpersonal skills.[7]

It is interesting to note that the phenomenon of victimising and demoralising teachers is not uncommon in nations that follow the market-model for education. We are mirroring the narrative of other Western nations. In the United States and the United Kingdom, commentators and media have engaged in the rhetoric of demonising teachers, blaming them alone for perceived falling standards. The conservative reform movement has led attacks on public education and favoured a move to small government and privatisation. Currently, Western developed nations appear to be influenced by the same movements and accompanying problems; while ignoring the evidence that identifies the real reasons for falling achievement levels.

> 'No calling in our society is more demanding than teaching; no calling in our society is more selfless than teaching; and no calling is more central to the vitality of a democracy than teaching.'
> – Roger Mudd

Working conditions

> 'Teachers are expected to teach unattainable goals with inadequate tools. The miracle is that at times they accomplish this impossible task.' – Dr Haim Ginott

If politicians are serious about attracting higher-quality candidates for teaching, they should realistically consider the remuneration levels offered. In 2012, the Productivity Commission released its report on Australia's workforce. The report found that 'a relatively low salary, for what has become an extremely complex and demanding job, lies at the heart of why teaching remains unattractive to most high achievers'.

The poor level of remuneration is becoming a consideration for young students contemplating their career choices. Recently an ex-student recognised me at the mall and while she professed fond memories of school she added, 'No offence, I would have considered teaching, but the pay is so poor compared to my other options at uni.'

As a point of interest, it has even been noted that teachers are paid one-tenth of babysitter fees.

To put it conversely, if the teaching profession attracted a salary comparable to other professions that require similar levels of training and responsibility, this would widen the options for those talented and suitable students who are deciding which direction to pursue.

Another concerning development is the attrition rate of the existing teaching workforce. Teacher morale has reached so low a point that many are considering alternative careers. Many feel undervalued and unappreciated. A recent study of the working conditions of Australian teachers revealed a number of alarming facts.[8] The survey found nearly two-thirds of teachers are considering quitting their jobs for a new career. An article from the US recounted the sad commentary of an ex-teacher. 'While she loved her first graders, her school was increasingly obsessed with standardised tests.' Her comment on reflection: 'It felt as though we were just teaching the kids how to fill in bubbles on exams.'[9]

Again, recent statistics reveal that one in three new teachers leave within the first three years after graduating.[10] Misty Adoniou, researcher and senior lecturer at the University of Canberra, studied a group of primary teaching graduates and found many felt disillusioned and disappointed. 'The big reason the teachers I was working with were talking about leaving was because they weren't able to do the teaching they'd been envisioning for not only all of their teaching degree, but many, many years before that as well.' Adoniou advocates mentoring as a crucial factor that assists new teachers. However, many who begin their career on contract, and are therefore often not assigned a secure position in a school, cannot benefit from mentoring. It should also be noted that it is not necessarily the less capable graduates that leave. The ACT branch secretary of the AEU adds, 'When you push teachers into being people who simply trot out lessons as prescribed for them and assess on external exams, they will run a mile. They need to be trusted.'

On a similar note, Pasi Sahlberg observed, 'Increased external control over teachers' work in schools through test-based accountability or centrally mandated regulation would likely deflect more bright, young people to professional areas where they have freedom to make use of their own creativity and initiative.'[11]

Two researchers from Monash University, Dr Paul Richardson and Dr Helen Watt, have been working on Australia's first longitudinal study since 2002, tracking teachers' careers, and they argue that chronic teacher shortages 'won't be solved as long as governments keep failing to confront the reasons why large numbers of teachers desert their jobs early'. The main reason cited is not poor pay but 'highly stressed, poor working conditions'. Twenty-seven per cent of teachers surveyed indicated they planned to quit teaching within their first five years of service. Many who had moved from other professions to teaching expressed 'shock at the working conditions and lack of administrative support'. In a comparison with other professions, '41% of teachers reported high levels of occupational stress compared with 31% of people in nursing, 29% in managerial jobs and 27% in professional and support management occupations'. Professor Tom Downes pointed out, 'When medical and law graduates come out into the workforce we make sure they have the simplest cases, they are carefully supervised when they do something, and the complex and really difficult cases are in the hands of the elite, most experienced practitioners. Teaching is one of the few professions where beginners are put into the deep end, almost thoughtlessly.'

Some members of the public believe teaching is an easy job. Just look at those hours, 9 to 3, and look at all those holidays! These people are hopelessly ignorant of the facts.

Anyone who knows a teacher, any parent who has helped out in the classroom, and any member of a teacher's family is fully aware of the struggle to maintain a work-life balance. Family time is certainly neglected or sacrificed when teachers are working late into the night and on weekends with preparation, planning and assessment. Teachers live on adrenalin. The work is often emotionally exhausting and the burn-out rate is high.

> 'School teachers are not fully appreciated by parents until it rains all day Saturday.' – E.C. McKenzie

It's obvious the critics don't stop to analyse the situation. How could anyone entertain, much less educate, a class of 25 to 30 energetic children without having prepared lessons for the day? How could they assess and report on their students' progress without dedicating an enormous amount of time and energy to conducting observations and checklists, consulting with colleagues and writing reports? Give these critics a two-hour birthday party with eight little boys and they would most likely collapse in a heap. These would be the same people you notice in the supermarket checkout queue at Christmas bemoaning the fact that school can't go back soon enough, as their children's frustration and boredom manifests in the form of a public tantrum.

Teaching is a profession that requires an enormous amount of stamina. It is physically and emotionally demanding. The school term breaks are a necessity, not a luxury. Both teachers and students start to exhibit burn-out symptoms of illness and tiredness towards the end of a ten-week term. Teachers who leave for other careers report that they don't miss the school holidays because their energy levels can be maintained. In an office position, you might be responsible for a staff of six independent adults, not thirty young children relying on your guidance and organisation skills. Interestingly, teachers notoriously become ill during school holidays. Perhaps it's because that is when they allow themselves to slow down and succumb. In fact, I used to refer to stand-down time as 'recuperation leave'.

So to enlighten the '9 to 3' critics, here is an account of a day in the life of a primary school teacher.

> 7.45 a.m. Arrive early for a team meeting; complete preparation for the morning activities; some photocopying; set up the interactive whiteboard; catch up with teaching partner and arrange to meet at recess to set up gym equipment in the hall; check emails; make sure pencils are sharpened, and rush to the toilet.
>
> There goes the bell. Jack's Mum wants to discuss issues regarding his progress. 'Sorry, I have to get to the class- can we meet after school? I have a staff meeting at 3.30 but could see you just after the children go.'
>
> They've settled into their first session. Oh, no. What's got into him? Perhaps he skipped breakfast. How did this little group of personalities end up in the same class? They'll have to be separated next year, if only for the teacher's sanity. It would be nice if we could get on with something constructive today; no interruptions.
>
> Guided reading time: 'Please don't disturb this group. You know

the routine.' By now they should be able to rotate between activities independently. Great – they're settled. Perhaps I have time for one running record while the rest are engaged. Poor little Matt; he struggles. 'Try again – you can do it – remember to look ahead and stretch out the word.' The beam on his face is worth it all.

Thank goodness; no recess duty today, but I won't get much time for lunch. Better check my emails while I have a second; grab a coffee; toilet break at last then rush to the gym to help set up the PE equipment.

They're used to gym rotations now and while it's very noisy, they're happy and active. I wish more could do up their own shoelaces. though!

Time for the IWB maths lesson. Isn't it amazing how a screen can captivate their attention? This little generation of screen kids – if it's not TV, it's computer games, iPads or mobile phones!

Lunchtime. Why do the food manufacturers make packets that children can't open? I'm glad I brought a sandwich – couldn't manage to gobble a salad while on playground duty. It's hardly conducive to digesting a meal in a relaxed atmosphere. I envy those teachers in some overseas countries whose governments have made provision for paid minders to take care of the students at play time. When you think of it, this isn't exactly part of their education, and what other professional has to mind other people's children in their lunch break?

Poor little Beth can't find a friend. 'How about you walk with me for a while?' 'Miss, Miss, he's cut his knee.' Hold on a second; fumble through the bum bag; past the list of alerts (kids with epilepsy, allergies to bee stings or peanuts; prone to anaphylactic shock); glad I did that professional development session on epi pens if I ever need to use one. Here's the first aid note. 'Are you his friend? Could you walk with him to the office?'

My replacement is five minutes late. Where is she? That leaves me just ten minutes to grab a quick cuppa and a quick trip to the bathroom. No wonder so many teachers suffer from urinary tract infections and kidney problems – not enough water and toilet stops!

Silent reading; bliss for a few minutes. Back to option 2 for the art class this afternoon. We'll use crayons – didn't get time to prepare paints.

3.05 p.m. 'Hello, Julie. What did you want to discuss about Jack?'

3.30 p.m. Staff meeting. Grab a cuppa and collapse into a chair; try to focus;

I just don't have the mental stamina for this right now. Someone's passing around a bowl of lollies; great, I need a sugar fix to get me through. Oh, don't argue the point; we'll be here till dark. (Perhaps we should try a standing meeting one day. I've heard they get through business much quicker).

5.45 p.m. Home at last. What did I leave out for dinner? 'How was your day? Have you guys done your homework yet?' Dad's home at last! 'Had a good day? Whose turn is it for dishes?'

I've only got some spelling and maths to mark tonight, thank goodness.

11 p.m. That's it! I can't do any more. Time for bed!

NB: Some super-human teachers claim they don't take work home. I don't know how they do it!

I remember one time feeling quite outraged watching an ignorant TV commentator brashly declaring, 'We just need to get more teachers out on the playground to stop the bullying.' His lack of awareness of teachers' working conditions was both frustrating and insulting as he berated teachers for expecting more than a five-minute break for lunch!

During a professional development session on behaviour management, I came to realise why teaching can be such a demanding, exhausting profession. The expert demonstrated that teachers are in 'control-mode', on full alert all day. Beneath the calm, controlled exterior, we are like meerkats constantly scanning, anticipating problems, pre-empting potential disputes, putting out spot fires. The adrenal glands are given a good work-out and, with few real breaks throughout the day, there is no down time until you actually get home.

To make matters worse, the burden of administrative tasks has escalated in recent years. When I began teaching, most of my effort and focus was directed to face-to-face teaching. Today, so much extra is expected of teachers, I would estimate face-to-face teaching might account for half the workload. The number of committees, meetings, professional development sessions, and admin report forms required leaves teachers exhausted and hampers their effort to be effective in the classroom.

I would speculate that the emphasis on accountability issues could be due to the increasingly litigious nature of our society. It has changed the nature of other professions as well. In recent years, there has been a noticeable lack of police visibility in the community and on the roads, while officers complete endless paperwork at the station. We don't see so many nurses tending to patients any more but there's always a team behind the desk filling out forms.

In fact, some circumstances have become quite ludicrous. There has been an increasing tendency to 'bubble-wrap' students for fear of being sued. In late 2012, Queensland teachers were required to do 'risk assessments' for activities including art and craft.[12] Paints and glues approved for use in schools obviously would not include toxins. The report added, 'Tiggy, handstands and running on bitumen have also been banned in some schoolyards over the past few years.' Measures such as these lead to an attitude of risk aversion in staff and in students. If children become anxious and are frightened of making mistakes, this will hinder learning and development.

In the ACT, several schools have cancelled their swimming carnivals in recent years because of concern about 'complying with heightened regulations and responsibilities for student safety'.[13] The new rules require teachers to assess all students and tag them before they can participate in any school swimming activity. The AEU commented that it was 'mindful of increasing teacher workloads and increasing community expectations as to what teachers should do'.

However, the prize for the most ridiculous ruling goes to a school in Essex, UK, where triangular flapjacks were banned after a boy was hit in the face by a flapjack. Flapjacks cut into squares and rectangles are still acceptable.[14]

On a more serious note, physical assaults on teachers are not uncommon. It's quite alarming to encounter union directives that indicate, 'For physical assaults have the member lodge three reports – Police report, Accident and Emergency report, and a Comcare Claim. Make sure they see their doctor immediately, take photos of any cuts or bruising and contact Injury Management.'[15]

In a study of working conditions of Australian teachers,[16] the survey found 'one third of Australia's state principals was physically attacked or witnessed physical violence in their workplace during 2011, and most of the violence involved aggressive parents'. This is not good enough.

Professional comparisons

> 'If a doctor, lawyer or dentist had forty people in his office at one time, all of whom had different needs, and some of whom didn't want to be there and were causing trouble, and the doctor, lawyer or dentist, without assistance, had to treat them all with professional excellence for nine months, then he might have some conception of the classroom teacher's job.' – Donald D. Quinn

What if we applied the same media attention and scrupulous examination of the quality of teachers to other professions?

We could have My Hospital, My Law Firm, My Media Outlet and My Politician websites and related league tables. Of course we would attach performance pay conditions as well and they would be measured by a series of narrow, inaccurate test results. What statistics would we use? Perhaps we could print how many patients experienced complications or died on the operating table; how many released criminals re-offended; how many political promises were broken or how many policies failed; and how many misreported articles or misleading stories or even outright lies were printed each day in newspapers and reported on television news channels.

No profession can claim that all of their members are of an exemplary standard. We can all recall high-profile cases where doctors have been struck off for misconduct, and politicians have been forced to resign after becoming embroiled in a scandal. Newspaper journalists have been found guilty of underhand practices such as phone hacking. Financial advisers have ripped off clients. Clergy have used their position of trust to abuse children. However, this does not imply that all members of any profession are guilty by association. Measuring the success of any profession is always going to be complicated. In the case of the medical profession, an experienced, more competent surgeon is assigned the more complex cases, and the very nature of these cases implies greater risk of complications.

Whenever the issue of media reform has been raised, those in power have countered the argument, raising the issue of freedom of speech. Broadcaster, author and academic Waleed Aly, however, has pointed out that the media is 'among the most unaccountable industries we have'.[17] There's a lack of competition due to a near monopoly of media ownership; the Press Council seems to have no real power; and self-regulation has proved to be ineffective. An outlandishly biased headline may later be retracted in small print at the back of the paper, but the first impression has had its impact. The damage has been done. When cornered, journalists often claim it was written as an 'opinion piece'. The general impression from the public is that the media has been discredited by its own actions.

It has always intrigued me why, for some perverse reason, some professions appear to be financially rewarded in inverse proportion to how they are valued by society. We are all familiar with the charts listing the most trusted professions. Up the top are paramedics, fire fighters, nurses, teachers and police officers. At the least trusted end of the scale we find financial advisers, lawyers, journalists, CEOs, bankers, celebrities, car salesmen, sex workers, politicians, telemarketers and real estate agents.[18]

Perhaps it's because society realises people drawn to a trusted-profession regard it as a vocation. They are not enticed primarily by the money on offer. Even so, when you analyse the function of a profession, I am still astounded by the massively disproportionate amount earned by movie stars or sporting celebrities when compared to teachers and nurses. A teacher's role is to educate and profoundly influence the next generation. Nurses and doctors take care of our health. The role of a movie star or sporting hero is primarily to entertain, perhaps inspire or provide an outlet for escape.

It is a sad commentary on our society if we truly place a higher value on entertainment over education and health. As an example, Nicole Kidman and Julia Roberts can command seventeen to twenty million dollars per movie. Actors Leonardo Di Caprio and Johnny Depp are worth fifty to seventy million dollars. When it was speculated that David Beckham was considering coming to Australia, it was estimated he could command two hundred thousand dollars per game.

Mike Duke, the CEO of Walmart, received a pay package in 2010 of 18.7 million dollars, yet he pays the average Walmart worker eleven dollars sixty cents an hour. As of May 2012, Gina Rinehart had amassed a personal fortune of 29.17 billion dollars, yet she vehemently campaigned against proposed mining taxes, to prevent the Australian population, who own the minerals, from sharing the benefits. The full extent of her attitude of entitlement was revealed when she commented wistfully that workers in Africa are willing to work for less than two dollars a day! The BBC estimated that while she was offering this advice she herself was earning six hundred dollars per second.[19] The latest OECD Better Life Index noted that in Australia 'there is a considerable gap between the richest and poorest – the top 20 per cent of the population earn six times as much as the bottom 20 per cent'.[20] A recent Oxfam report states, 'the richest 85 people across the globe share a combined wealth of one trillion pounds, as much as the poorest 3.5 billion of the world's population'.[21] To help visualise these figures, the report noted that those eighty-five people could squeeze onto a single double-decker bus.

Bill Gates advocates that the wealthy have a civic duty to share some of their wealth. They did not get rich on their own. As Elizabeth Warren, the US Massachusetts Senator so eloquently put it, 'You built a factory out there? Good for you… But…you moved your goods to market on the roads the rest of us paid for. You hired workers the rest of us paid to educate. You were safe in your factory because of police forces and fire forces that the rest of us paid for.'[22] A 2011 OECD report warned that growing inequity is undermining economic growth, and unless this is addressed it 'will affect economic performance as a whole'.

It is interesting to note where politicians are placed on the trust chart. Sometimes I feel I would be reluctant to take a group of schoolchildren to view a parliamentary session. They are too unruly, rude, inconsiderate and disrespectful. And I'm not referring to the students. In class, students are taught about what constitutes 'audience behaviour'. They're taught to take turns, to listen when somebody else is speaking and to show respect and consideration. On most sitting days, that's not what is on display in our parliament. Frequent shouting, jeering, bullying, and ignoring the speaker is often what we see from the 'Honourable Members'.

Yet politicians are awarded automatic pay rises, without having to trade conditions or forfeit pay for strike action after the EBA discussions have been delayed for months. They justify the situation with the notion that it is necessary in order to attract higher-quality candidates and they often refer to the quote, 'If you pay peanuts you can expect monkeys.' Interestingly, this principle doesn't seem to apply to other professions.

Already the wages of my adult children in government jobs have exceeded my final salary after thirty years of working as a teacher. A September 2008 OECD report on spending concluded, 'The highest wage for Australian teachers is significantly lower than in most other developed nations, despite teachers here working longer hours and having bigger classes.'[23]

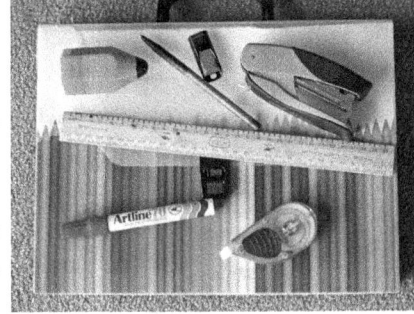

Add to this the teachers' habit of often spending a significant amount of their own money on their class and on professional development courses, much to the chagrin of their spouses.[24]

> Teaching – the only profession where you steal supplies from home and bring them to work.

So while salary levels are not a primary incentive for teachers, being recognised and awarded appropriate remuneration would certainly be appreciated. Dan Buettner, in his book *Thrive*, offers the following career advice: 'Choose bliss over bucks.' My question is why they should be considered incompatible.[25]

So if teachers are prepared to work with difficult conditions and poor pay, what is it that primarily motivates them? Most teachers are drawn to the career because they genuinely believe they can make a difference. And the satisfaction they derive comes from intrinsic rewards.

Intrinsic rewards

> 'Thousands of candles can be lighted from a single candle, and the life of the candle will not be shortened.' – Buddha

The intense satisfaction of helping children achieve a breakthrough in their learning cannot be measured or bought. That special moment when their eyes light up and their little faces beam; when they're nearly bursting with pride; the satisfaction they display in their own achievements; and the enthusiasm that accompanies their efforts to succeed; those moments when their personalities blossom and their confidence grows: these are the intrinsic rewards teachers can relate to.

Teachers who work with older students would experience appreciation in a different form, but early childhood teachers treasure the little letters we receive from our students, knowing how proud they are to be able to express themselves in writing. Many declare, 'You're the best teacher in the world', and while their sentiments are genuine, you know that next year's teacher will receive the same devotion and be awarded that title too.

Letters of appreciation from parents also mean a lot to teachers. It is both satisfying and gratifying for parents to acknowledge your contribution to their child's development.

People could not be drawn to teaching if they did not genuinely like children. I enjoy the company of children. I appreciate their refreshing approach to thinking and learning; their unique way of looking at the world with open minds; their astonished delight at discovering something new; their pure energy; and their positive approach to life. I admire their honesty. When you receive a compliment from a child, you know it's genuine. They can lift your spirits when they tell you that you look pretty today. Their criticisms are equally honest. A little girl once asked me if I forgot to brush my hair. I told her, 'No, I paid a hairdresser a lot of money to look like this.'

Sarcasm is wasted on children. They interpret everything literally. Once a rather perplexed little boy asked in astonishment why I had exclaimed, 'Oh, great!' when something went wrong. Children don't have the capacity to be jaded or cynical. However, they are good judges of character and they sense immediately when adults' intentions are not genuine or when they are being condescending.

We could learn a lot from children. There is no limit to their imagination. They have the ability to suspend their disbelief and escape into the world of make-believe and I think it's a great pity many adults have forgotten how to play.

Adults are often amused by the quirky nature of how children process information. Over the years, I have amassed many anecdotes and stories that demonstrate their novel approach. Their questions can be logical yet sometimes absurd. 'Where do bubbles go when they burst?' 'Why do men have nipples?' 'How do birds sleep'? 'Why do dogs wag their tails?' 'How do worms dig holes in the ground?' 'What makes a seed grow?'

My parents and a couple of their neighbours and friends helped out with Grandparents' Day at my school one year. Little Sammy, who had never seen someone quite so old, gazed up at my mother's friend and inquired, 'Are you dead yet?' Fortunately, she was not offended and recounted the tale many times.

Cameron was feeling unwell one day, so I sent him to the sick bay. He complained of 'a pain in the lungs'. When he returned fifteen minutes later, he handed me a note from the first-aid officer. 'Cameron suspects breast cancer. Hmm, I'll let him rest for five minutes and send him back.'

On Harmony Day we passed around a box with a mirror hidden inside. The children were told the secret inside would reveal the most important person in the world. Most peeped in, smiled and passed it on. However, Seamus began flapping his arms, repeating excitedly, 'Oh, I know, I know…' But when he received the box the excitement drained form his face and was replaced by a wave of utter dismay. Curious and a little alarmed, I asked him what he had thought was inside the box. 'God' was his reply. I was astounded but also flattered that he thought I could possibly deliver God in a box.

These few anecdotes demonstrate that to understand how children learn you have to understand how they think, and appreciate the world through their eyes. Teachers continue to tolerate excessive workloads and less than ideal working conditions because they are dedicated to their clients, the students. Teaching is not just a job, it's a vocation. It is both a responsibility and a privilege to be given such a position of trust; to have such a significant influence on the next generation. While genuine recognition of their worth would go a long way to improving

teacher morale, what teachers really want in return for their efforts is to feel appreciated, respected, supported and valued by society.

'A teacher somewhere in your neighbourhood tonight is grading and preparing lessons to teach your children while you are watching television. In the minute it takes you to read this, teachers all over the world are using their "free" time, and often their own money, for your child's literacy, prosperity and future.' While this popular Internet comment about commitment and dedication may also apply to other professions, it would certainly resonate with may teachers.

5

The Role of the Parent

> 'If you raise your children to feel that they can accomplish any goal or task they decide upon, you will have succeeded as a parent and you will have given your children the greatest of all blessings.' – Brian Tracy

There is a commonly held misconception that schools should accept sole responsibility for a child's education, but teachers believe education is a shared responsibility. Parents and teachers are partners in a child's education. That might sound clichéd, but it is a relationship that is absolutely vital for the success of a child's education.

Parents are the child's first teachers. Before they enter school, children have learnt to walk, to talk and to socialise. The parents' influence during those formative years is critical. When parents hand their children over to the preschool or kindergarten teacher, they are entrusting them with a profound responsibility, and while they may have faith in the teacher's ability, the children's development is enhanced when parents remain engaged with the school.

An opinion survey of teachers conducted by National Excellence in Teaching Awards (NEiTA) and the Australian Scholarship Group (ASG) culminated in a list of key points concerning parental responsibilities:

- teach your child respect, acceptable behaviour, good manners, personal hygiene, punctuality, and healthy choices.
- teach your child the importance of values and morals.
- teachers think the areas of sexuality, drug education and personal safety issues, including water, road and energy safety, are parental responsibilities.

- encourage positive attitudes, especially with older children.
- allow your child to make mistakes and accept responsibility for their own actions.[1]

In a recent report, analysis conducted by the Australian Alliance for Children and Youth 'confirms high levels of community and parental engagement [have] a major impact on a child's school education success'.[2] It follows that children who are encouraged and supported at home experience greater academic success. The latest international analysis of elements of success in education found 'Students' motivation and engagement can have a profound impact on their classroom performances in the short term and can affect the quality of their learning in the long term.'[3]

Effective communication results in a shared understanding of the roles of parents and teachers. A balanced level of parental involvement produces the best results. Concern in recent years about 'helicopter parents' led to formal guidelines clarifying issues such as appropriate times to contact teachers, and reasonable expectations of responses and actions to requests.

One of the most important qualities of the parent–teacher relationship is mutual respect. When parents demonstrate respect for their child's teacher, the child is more likely to respect the teacher also.

Talk-back radio often reflects societal values. I noticed a common theme both in Australia and Canada where parents queried the success of students from Asian families. When you examine values it becomes evident that parents of Asian background place a very high value on education and hold teachers in high esteem. They actively encourage their children to work to the best of their ability. If parents really want their child to succeed, they must demonstrate by example that they value education.

The list below was displayed on a wall at a local school:

1. Children are more likely to be achievers if their parents join together to give the same clear and positive message about school effort and expectations.

2. Children can learn appropriate behaviours more easily if they have an effective model to imitate.

3. Communication about a child between adults(referential speaking) dramatically affects children's behaviour.

4. Overreactions by parents to children's success or failures leads them to feel either intense pressure to succeed or despair and discouragement in dealing with failure.

5. Children feel more tension when they are worrying about their work than when they are doing that work.

6. Children develop self-confidence through struggle.

7. Deprivation and excess frequently exhibit the same symptoms.

8. Children develop confidence and an internal sense of control if power is given to them in gradually increasing increments as they show maturity and responsibility.

9. Children become oppositional if one adult allies with them against a parent or a teacher, making them more powerful than an adult.

10. Adults should avoid confrontations with children unless they are sure they can control the outcomes.

11. Children will become achievers only if they learn to function in competition.

12. Children will continue to achieve if they usually see the relationship between the learning process and its outcomes.[4]

> 'Tots who started kindergarten at a certain elementary school came home the first day with a special note from the teachers which read, in part, "If you promise not to believe everything your child says happens at school, I'll promise not to believe everything he says happens at home."' – Harry B. Otis

The race

We have become a generation of 'road runners', beep-beeping our way through life. In reaction to elements of modern life, such as fast food, the 'slow movement' has evolved. An active proponent, Carl Honore has written a book, *In Praise of Slowness*. Honore is known as the ambassador of the Slow Parenting Movement. In a recent documentary, *Frantic Family Rescue*, he conducted an experiment with three families, offering them a 'slow-fix'. Honore challenged all members of the families to turn off screens and reduce the scheduled, organised and structured extracurricular activities they were engaged in after school and on weekends. He encouraged them to eat meals together. Most involved in the experiment appreciated the benefits of slowing down. In the documentary Honore refers to the habit of 'hyper-parenting' and explains that slow is about 'striking a balance, finding time for one-to-one interaction and improving the quality of family life.'

Arianna Huffington, in her book *Thrive*, also warns us of the phenomenon of 'hurry sickness' in our society. She advocates the health benefits of slowing down and also ensuring we all get enough sleep. Huffington quotes psychiatry professor Vatal Thakker of the NYU School of Medicine, whose work suggests a strong link between hyperactivity and children with sleep disorders. He notes that 'Sleep is especially crucial for children who need the deep, slow-wave type of sleep called delta sleep' and believes children of today are getting far less sleep than children of past generations. Huffington suggests, 'It's about changing how we over-schedule our children's days so that they can begin their nights sooner.'[5]

Life is not a race. Who wants to get to the end first? So why should schooling be considered a race? The American education program Race To The Top was given a very unfortunate name, and it appears they didn't succeed. In education, it is not a case of he who gets there first wins. In fact, racing ahead can have quite the opposite effect. Throughout Australia there are different cut-off dates in each of the states for school-entry age. Generally a child's formal schooling begins at age five, a full two years before children in Scandinavian countries.

Ben Edwards, from the Australian Institute of Family Studies, has been conducting a longitudinal study of Australian children.[6] He found that there is a general perception that boys benefit from delayed entry. Researchers have also noticed a recent trend for parents to delay entry to school, many believing it could make the difference between coping and thriving. The older starting age does appear to offer distinct social and emotional advantages.

Ultimately, the decision should be based not only on age, but on the level of maturity and learning readiness. Attempting to accelerate learning without securing a consolidated base will not achieve lasting success.

Modern society does appear to have an obsession with fast-tracking life. People have created programs that tell you, 'Your Baby Can Read'. They have promoted baby beauty salons, and there is a trend to sexualise little girls' fashion. As a result, the fashion industry has contributed to body image disorders in children as young as eight.

Once at school, many children are then enrolled in after-school tutoring programs. This is very popular with new Australians who have left their country of origin for a better life and naturally want their children to excel. However, sometimes I wonder if the motivation is a matter of 'catch up' or 'get ahead'? Either way, the programs do not deliver on their promises long-term. They might achieve short-term results with the advantage of one-to-one tutoring compared with regular class sizes of twenty to twenty-five, but their rote-learning methods rarely result in meaningful understanding of concepts. There is also the risk of a common, unintended consequence when children resent the extra work and learning becomes a chore. These businesses thrive in the current environment; not so the children.

On a Saturday morning in a city mall in Singapore, you are likely to come across a room of children undertaking extra classes. While visiting one year, my attention was drawn to an article in Singapore's *Sunday Times*.[7] The story investigated the trend towards enrichment lessons for kindergarten children, designed to give them a head-start for primary school. So, as well as kinder classes five days a week, these six-year-olds attend 'English, mathematics and 'mother-tongue' classes once or twice a week'. This is very popular despite advice from experts such as Phua Kia Wang, the principal of North Vistar Primary, who stated, 'It is not advisable for children to go to tuition which teaches them beyond their developmental readiness. This may cause children to be unduly anxious because they are unable to cope.'

There is heated debate currently in the US about the wisdom or otherwise of the Common Core State Standards (CSSS) that insist with kindergarten students that there is an expectation that *all* children should learn to read in kindergarten, when many are clearly not developmentally prepared. This political push ignores early childhood expertise and has led to inappropriate classroom practices.

Even locally there is a trend to get swept up in the race and push ahead without any real thought or direction. A colleague who returned to teaching after spending a few years at home with young children found vastly different expectations in the education system. Expositions, one of the text-types she had been teaching Year 4 previously, were now expected to be covered in Year 2. Five years ago, kindergarten children were expected to reach a reading benchmark of level five; now it's level eight.

Disregarding students' level of maturity and understanding is counterproductive. The questions need to be asked, why are we doing this? Where is the pressure coming from? Who are we trying to impress? Who are we competing with? What is the purpose of it? In Finland, with a school starting age of seven, children consistently outrank Australia in the international PISA test, and they don't appear to be racing anybody.

I should clarify the difference between early intervention and early entry at school. If a genuine delay is identified, there is a definite and beneficial case for early intervention. Specifically targeted and designed programs to improve prospects help prevent further delay. In many cases, if left unchecked, the condition could lead to further complications which are more difficult and costly to correct retrospectively. For example, if a three-year-old child is identified with a speech delay, he would need to see a speech therapist now. Being told there is a two-year waiting list is not uncommon. By the time the child is five years old, the problem has compounded and is twice as difficult to rectify.

Equally important is the necessity to recognise gifted and talented students. Often students with exceptional talents, and not necessarily academic talents, go unnoticed and vital opportunities are missed. Many times these are the students who become distracted in class because they are not being challenged and inspired.

The fear campaign and parental anxiety

The international terrorism events of 11 September and the Bali bombings helped create a climate of fear within society. Repeated images of the disasters were indelibly imprinted on our minds by the media frenzy that followed. We were advised to be alert, not alarmed.

It is not uncommon for governments to use the threat of terrorism as a political tool. The use of the 'fear card' is a well-known tactic designed to enhance the incumbent's position while deflecting attention and scrutiny from domestic issues and policies. While it would be reckless to ignore the rise of the brutal Islamic State militants in the Middle East, the current hysteria over the threat of terrorism locally does appear extreme. While we were not assigned a dedicated Minister for Science, the federal government created a position of Minister Assisting the Prime Minister on Counter Terrorism.

In modern Western populations, it seems many people drive around cities in large jeeps; they isolate themselves with home theatre systems; and install security devices to protect their property and their computer files. We have seen the development of gated communities designed to protect residents from the outside world.

This general uneasiness seems to have permeated family life. During the previous decade, the 'school choices' issue divided the community. Those who could afford private school fees often stated that one of the reasons for enrolling their children in private schools was to isolate them from troubled sections of the population. Subtle and not-so-subtle pressure was exerted on parents to seriously consider whether they were doing enough for their children. It continues today.

An advertisement on the back of some Canberra buses features a photo of a little girl in a school uniform, and the question is posed: 'Does Your Child Come First?' The implication is, if you are not prepared to make large sacrifices and send your child to this private Christian college, then society will judge you as inadequate. This is a business advertising its product, using marketing techniques that attempt to manipulate parental insecurities.

In a local government school where I frequently work, there is a large population of children with special needs. Some have varying degrees of autism and others have a variety of disabilities. I find the majority of children at the school have benefited and gained life skills by being part of this inclusion policy in practice. They tend to be more accepting and tolerant of differences and are able to display a great deal of empathy. They understand that if one student is allowed to play with a squishy toy while they are all engaged in a listening activity, it is because he has different needs.

> 'Public schools are one of the first places where kids learn a life-long lesson: how to get along with people from different walks of life.' – Sandra Feldman

Work/life balance and the influence on family stress[8]

There is no shortage of statistics to confirm Australians now work some of the longest working hours in the developed world. 'Full-time employees are working an average of 44 hours per week. In international standards we've got some of the longest full-time working hours among the OECD.'[9] An Australia Institute study from 2009 found Australia's long working hours surpassed even Japan's, and another study claimed we work the second longest hours in the world after Korea.

Professor Alan Duncan, from the Income and Wealth Report: Race Against Time,[10] found that Australian full-time work hours have increased by almost three hours for men and two hours for women since 1985. 'These types of work patterns have potentially adverse affects on family life, a greater requirement for tag-team parenting and add time pressures that working couples particularly are feeling.' He added, 'Balancing work and family life remains a big issue for Australian men and women, with around 40% of women and 30% of men feeling often or always pushed or pressured for time.'

While I was completing my degree in the mid-1970s, one unit of my sociology major was titled Sociology of Work. The theory at the time was that with the development of technology there would be more leisure time in the future and we would have to learn how to manage our leisure time. It didn't happen! In fact, an Adelaide survey on stress[11] estimated the average worker worked so much unpaid overtime, they were actually donating seventeen to nineteen days' free labour per year to their employers. Unfortunately, the longer working hours have not been matched with increased productivity, which implies we are working harder but not smarter, and at the expense of a balanced family life.

Why is this happening and what are the consequences for family life? As well as dealing with the high cost of housing, we have become the ultimate consumers. Advertisers have effectively convinced us that our wants are actually our needs. We have been engaging in 'retail therapy' in the belief that this will make us happy and solve all our problems. Current news cycles constantly remind us that retailers are hurting because, after the global financial crisis occurred, consumers actually started to put away their credit cards and save.

In her book *The Work/Life Collision*, Barbara Peacock describes the work-earn-consume cycle that has been tipping us off balance. To accentuate the situation, certain governments have proposed we trade holidays for higher levels of pay, which would result in increased levels of stress and less time and energy for family life. This in turn would affect children's learning and ultimate success.

So what can be done about the situation? Research by the University of South Australia suggests more flexible working arrangements, such as the ability to work from home or agreeing on different working hours, might help adjust the work–life balance, and also, according to evidence, 'lead to higher productivity, better motivation, and increased loyalty among staff'.[12] The study also claims, 'increased flexibility benefits both employee and employer, and is associated with lower work-life conflict, improved performance, reduced absenteeism and health benefits.'

Over-scheduling and helicopter parents

In 2009, Scott Harper produced an ABC documentary titled *Lost Adventures of Childhood*. The program included many statistics which encapsulate modern family life:

– Canadian children spend ninety per cent of their days indoors.

– The radius of play of the average nine-year-old has shrunk to one-ninth of what it was in 1970.

– Time spent in organised sport has more than doubled since 1981.

– Forty-one per cent of kids aged nine to thirteen say they feel stressed all of the time.

– Worldwide prescriptions for Ritalin, Attenta and Focalin have tripled since 1993.

– Two-thirds of British kids aged eight to ten have never played outside on their own.

This scenario has been brought about in the current generation by parental fear; fear for a child's safety and fear of falling behind.

In the 1950s and 60s, free-range kids headed out to play in the neighbourhood in the morning. They often had lunch wherever they happened to be at lunchtime. Parents would keep a look out for each other's children, and the rule was 'Be back home for tea.' This was in the days when people didn't bother to lock their doors and trust was not a major issue. This is not simply a nostalgic view of the past but, as the program indicated, it is a commentary on how society has changed and a reflection on what children have lost in the process.

Statistically, the world has not become less safe, yet over the past twenty years a wave of parental anxiety over the safety of children has created a modification of lifestyle. Children are more supervised, restricted and monitored. They have lost the freedom of childhood play.

In some cases, parents use tracking devices to monitor their children's movements. Daily updated photographs of kids at summer camp are available via the internet for parents to scrutinise, and web cams are used for surveillance in day care centres. This demonstrates a lack of trust of children and of society. Not surprisingly, parental fear and apprehension is transferred to the children. If we continue down this path, I wonder if we might end up micro-chipping our children as we do our pets.

Some children are so over-scheduled with before and after school and weekend activities that they are suffering from anxiety. The documentary interviewed young children attending therapy centres for stress management. A common complaint from the little participants was 'I only get to rest one day a week.'

We would all be familiar with the story of Tiger Mom Amy Chua, who forced her daughters to practise piano for hours and would not allow them to 'waste time'. When her girls become adults, it would be interesting to follow up the effects of such an overambitious, authoritarian style of parenthood.

When our children were young, we gave them opportunities to engage in extra-curricular activities including soccer, little athletics, basketball, puppetry and ballet. Fortunately for us, they were very much homebodies and preferred to play with their friends at home. We insisted they finish what they had committed to but did not demand they continue beyond that. The activity that maintained our girl's interest was ballet, and that was partly due to the relaxed attitude of the ballet teacher. She realised what appealed to her little students was music, dance, beautiful costumes and lots of fun. One little friend attending another local ballet school injured her Achilles tendon after being pressured by a teacher with quite a different agenda, perhaps hoping to discover a star to enhance her own reputation.

Carl Honore, the proponent of the Slow Parenting Movement and author of *Under Pressure*, spent two years studying children's play and the state of childhood in Europe, Asia and North and South America. He commented, 'Modern parents push to give their children the best of everything and make them the best at everything. It seems children would benefit if life was more balanced; if sometimes we just let children be children; and if sometimes we just let them play.'

> 'It's paradoxical that many educators and parents still differentiate between a time for learning and a time for play without seeing the vital connection between them.' – Leo F. Buscaglia

Play fulfils a vital role in all species. If you observe baby animals, you see that the most natural activity is for them to engage in play. There is a reason for this. They learn through play. When children engage in spontaneous, unstructured, unsupervised play, they gain life skills. Through their interaction, they learn about communication, cooperation, creative problem-solving, conflict resolution and risk management. They also gain many other social and emotional developmental skills, including self-confidence and resilience.

'Helicopter parents' endeavour to protect their children from experiencing difficulties. This leads to a habit of risk aversion. Parents and teachers need to reassure children that it's OK to make a mistake. In fact, we often learn the most meaningful lessons from our mistakes. Children need to know that in life, while each person is a unique individual, there is only one winner in a race. It could be due to talent or hard work, or it could be through luck; and we need to understand that if we're not the one who won, then perhaps we need to try harder next time.

I am guilty of this also. At our children's birthday parties, I would wrap a small surprise in each layer of Pass the Parcel. The music wasn't stopped randomly. I ensured that each child received a prize. But when I thought about my own experience as a kid at birthday parties, the excitement of the game was enhanced by the unpredictability of who would end up with the last piece of wrapping paper with the prize inside.

Amanda Ripley, an American journalist who studied the world's education superpowers, found that a common focus on rigour was a significant element that contributed to success.[13] She noted that through our obsession with promoting self-esteem, children have realised that they are not always genuinely expected to earn praise. Our attempts to protect egos often lead to risk aversion, and this in turn is detrimental to success.

According to Kath Walker, author of *What's the Hurry?*, raising children is about nurturing, not training; encouraging, not controlling; modelling and setting boundaries and rules.

Screen kids: the flip side of over-scheduling

> 'By the age of seven, a child born in Britain today will have spent an entire year (8,766 hours) of his or her life looking at TV, computer and game console screens. By thirteen it will be three whole years.'[14]

There is a general awareness that children are spending more time in front of screens. While there are some cognitive benefits with computer games, the fact is, instant gratification from access to the internet does not equate to knowledge and understanding. It does not promote deeper thinking. The amount of time individuals spend sitting alone, not interacting with others, is affecting their social skills. Even while watching TV, a family is often sitting together and interacting to some extent.

When too much time is spent on social networking sites, there is no eye contact, physical contact or component of human interaction. There is no subconscious monitoring of body language through non-verbal cues and therefore the concern is that children are not developing the skills essential for empathy. Psychologist Sherry Turkle, in her recent book *Alone Together: Why We Expect More From Technology and Less From Each Other*, argues, 'the more consciously connected people are in cyberspace, the more isolated they feel'.[15]

Baroness Susan Greenfield, a neuroscientist and researcher at Oxford University, agrees.[16] She claims people living in a two-dimensional world, who claim they have hundreds of friends on Facebook, are deluding themselves. These are superficial relationships and cannot be compared with real-life close friendships in which people interact in a meaningful way. If we encourage children to use their screens excessively, we are impeding their social and emotional development and their learning opportunities.

Ironically named, our smart phones are not making us any smarter. Our insatiable need for inter-connectedness is almost an addiction, particularly so for teenagers. If challenged to turn off all our devices even for a week, would we be able to contemplate it?

The Sydney Myopia Study found in 2015 that 'The

academic hot-housing of children as they spend too much time poring over books and screens inside, is ruining their eyesight.'[17] Over the past fifteen years myopia levels have risen from 20% to 30% in seventeen-year-olds, and 'between 2005 and 2011 the proportion of 12 year olds with myopia increased from 4% to 9% in Caucasians and from 39% to 53% in Asian children.' The study suggests a combination of intensive study habits and excessive use of screen devices could be exacerbating eyesight problems, along with lack of outdoor time.[17]

Of course, the other obvious detrimental effect of too much screen time is inactivity, which is contributing to the looming obesity epidemic. A Deakin University study in 2009 found preschoolers were spending eighty-five per cent of their waking hours inactive. No doubt the figures would we worse now.[18] The findings are comparable with results from international studies, and even more alarming was the fact that physical activity declines throughout childhood. We just need to remember: more time spent in front of a screen is time not spent doing other things. Activities such as skipping, hopping, rolling, jumping and kneading dough help to strengthen neural pathways whereas screens provide a passive input.

So while screens are revolutionising education, because of the inbuilt addictive qualities of computer games, Dr Kate Highfield, a lecturer at the Institute of Early Childhood at Macquarie University, suggests parents should regulate screen time. They should carefully select suitable apps and monitor and limit the amount of time devoted to being in front of a screen.[19]

The homework debate

Homework has always been a subject of debate. To evaluate the worth of any undertaking, we need to ask what its purpose is and whether it achieves that purpose. To say we've always done things this way is not a justification. Some cite the benefits as developing organisational and research skills and good study habits. However, most experts find that, especially in the early grades, homework can actually have a detrimental effect on a child's attitude to school work. Professor Richard Walker, co-author of *Reforming Homework: Practices, Learning and Policies* with

Mike Horsley, believes that 'homework of the uninspiring form that is most common (worksheets) is of little benefit. Except with those in Years 11 and 12, there is definite evidence to show that homework is of no benefit when it comes to improving academic achievement.'[20]

John Hattie, the director of the Melbourne Research Institute at the University of Melbourne agrees. 'Homework as it is usually undertaken is likely to have little or no effect in primary schools.'[21]

Those who oppose homework say it impinges on family life and adds to stress in the family. Children need to unwind and relax after school, or perhaps engage in sport or some other activity that motivates them. Traditional homework consisting of photocopied sheets further accentuates the sedentary nature of modern life.

Many parents can't see the point of the tasks set and, in today's busy world, they resent the time involved. It is often a major cause of conflict in the household, as commented by parents Anita and John during a news item on the topic: 'In fact, it's the bane of our family life'; and after all, we all know that it's often the parents who are completing the homework in any case!

Child psychologist Michael Carr-Gregg believes, 'It's hijacking family life, it's bound to cause arguments and it's turning kids into couch potatoes.'[22] This view is supported by Dr Ian Lillico, educational consultant and founder of the Boys Forward Institute and author of *The Homework Grid*. He would prefer any set homework to consist of interactive learning opportunities such a family game of Scrabble or a visit to the theatre.

I have even encountered homework set for preschoolers, the reason given being that it was school policy to set homework. The teachers were required to create homework on top of the basic expectation that parents would be regularly reading to their children. So they devised tasks around family chores. They received some negative feedback, and justifiably so. Why would teachers prescribe domestic chores or family relationships and interactions?

Schools need to examine their reasons for setting homework. If the main reason is to appease a vocal minority of parents, then that is not a good enough reason.

For those parents who feel homework is necessary, perhaps they should negotiate with their children's teachers to set meaningful, worthwhile assignments with some degree of choice. If children have choice, they are more likely to invest genuine effort and gain some satisfaction from the exercise.

When our son was in high school, he used to bemoan the fact that his mate's parents paid him ten dollars for every A he achieved. I tried to explain that it was not a good enough incentive to try to please others and that the motivation should come from his sense of satisfaction with his own achievements. When his friend prematurely dropped out of high school, he realised that intrinsic rewards were the only ones that would sustain effort and success.

The best homework habit is to encourage your children to read, read and read!

Parents' roles and responsibilities

To sum up, there is a perception that schools aren't doing enough, despite the overcrowded curriculum. When it comes to basic values and morals, these principles do belong with parents and families. When you see children behaving badly in public places such as shopping malls, and the parents warn them, 'School will sort you out!', they should reconsider. Good behaviour is modelled at home. How we treat other people is modelled at home; and children are good imitators.

Some things to do

Spend quality time with your children. It's more precious to them than any expensive toy.

Provide a positive role model by reading books, magazines and so on at home so children regard reading as a natural, enjoyable pastime.

Read to your children often so they associate reading with happy, cosy and positive memories. Treat books as treasures.

Provide your children with challenges, and allow them to fail. They will learn their best lessons from their own mistakes.

If you are planning to travel overseas or around Australia, embrace the opportunity. The children can express their impressions of relevant and meaningful experiences in creative journal writing. What they will gain from the experience in first-hand learning and life skills will be invaluable.

Teach your children to swim. It could save their lives.

Teach your children to tie their shoelaces. Take pity on teachers trying to assist twenty-five children with shoelaces after a gym session.

Set high expectations for your children's behaviour

Allow and encourage your children to be involved in cooking. It might be messy but they can gain so much from the experience.

Take the time to make nutrition a top priority. It not only affects your children's health but it also has a direct impact on achievement at school.

Read all labels on processed food. Additives and preservatives can interfere with learning.

Dare to say No to your children when it's appropriate. They feel more secure with set limits and boundaries.

Prioritise your own health. Tired, cranky and stressed parents are in no condition to provide support and encouragement – the qualities that help children to develop and learn.

Show that you respect your partner. Be a team. As the saying goes, 'The most important thing a father can do for his children is to love their mother.'

Some things *not* to do

Don't teach your children to read by sounding out individual letter sounds. When they're ready and able to look ahead and recognise groups of letters or whole words, they will see that 'ea' as in 'beach' doesn't sound like 'e' as in egg, 'a' as in ant, and 'ch' doesn't sound like 'c' as in cat and 'h' as in hat.

Don't teach your children to spell their names in upper case (capital) letters. It's much harder to unlearn habits than to learn the correct way initially.

Don't over-schedule your children's every waking moment with before/after school and week end activities. Both you and your children will benefit from a better work/life balance.

Don't allow too much screen-time.

Don't hassle your children over homework. Don't allow it to become a source of family conflict.

Don't waste your money on expensive toys. So often children have more fun playing with the boxes they came in.

Don't expect schools to undo firmly established bad behaviour.

Don't contradict your partner in front of the children. They're very perceptive and they'll use it against you.

Similarly, don't undermine your children's teachers in front of the children.

Don't allow other people to judge your parenting skills and undermine your confidence.

6

Finland

Let's look at a place where the education system is working well. We will examine how it was designed and how it differs from our approach.

Finland is often quoted as having the most successful education system in the world. Finland's students consistently perform at the top of an international test known as PISA (the Program for International Student Assessment). The test is sponsored by the OECD and it examines ability in reading, science and mathematics skills. It is administered every three years to fifteen-year-old students in sixty-five developed countries (2009). Researchers and experts from around the world frequently visit Finland to study the education system, to learn from and determine which elements contribute to the successful academic achievement of Finnish students.

Finland didn't always have one of the best education systems in the world. Twenty-five years ago, it was ranked well behind places like USA and UK. So what happened? Their success can be attributed to a combination of inter-related elements. To determine the development of their success we need to examine their history, the shared cultural values, the vital role played by teachers, and the teaching and assessment methods that have been adopted. The process of education reform was developed over decades and was due to many factors and influences.

Historical factors

After the upheaval of World War II, Finland strove for unification through a process of reform. The transformation from a poor agriculture and timber-based country to a modern, high-tech knowledge-based society with an excellent education system was not simply a happy coincidence. During that period there were three economic and political influences that contributed to change. The collapse of the Soviet Union helped Finland consolidate its identity. The country then survived a recession in the early 1990s, identifying opportunity and taking a new direction, investing in research and development and innovation. When Finland joined the EU (1992–1995), this also signified a new direction and identity.

Pasi Sahlberg, Director General of the Centre for International Mobility (CIMO) at the Finnish Ministry of Education and Culture, credits the education system as 'the key driver that raised the nation out of the economic crisis'.[1] Education was seen as an investment, not a cost, and the strong focus on mathematics, science and technology, together with a focus on research and innovation, led to the success of companies such as Nokia (in mobile communications) and Stora Enso (in paper manufacturing). During that period, the Finns studied and analysed education policies of other countries, including the UK and USA, and adopted successful elements. They moved from the old system of grammar schools and civic schools to a comprehensive, inclusive basic school system, known as peruskoulu. Commonly valued elements included equality of opportunity; the importance of cooperation and collaboration; research-based training for teachers; and a focus on the potential of each individual. Teaching became regarded as a prominent and highly prestigious profession.

The school system

In Finland, children begin their formal education at seven years of age. The nine-year comprehensive school system, peruskoulu, encompasses a child-centred, holistic approach. School and class sizes are small and are governed by local authorities. Teachers are guided by a national curriculum but are encouraged to individualise programs to meet the needs of students. After the age of sixteen, students choose whether to attend an academic upper secondary or vocational school.

Basic compulsory subjects are studied in the upper secondary schools. However, since the 1990s, age-cohort groupings of students have been replaced with a more flexible system allowing greater choice of subjects. After upper secondary education, students are eligible to take the national matriculation examination and they may pursue continued studies at higher education institutions.

The teaching profession

Pasi Sahlberg believes, 'Without excellent teachers and a modern teacher-education system, Finland's current international achievement would have been impossible.' In Finland, teaching is considered as prestigious a profession as that of a medical practitioner or a lawyer. Teacher selection is highly competitive, with training involving a research-based university master's degree taking five to seven years. Applicants are required to have high academic scores and strong interpersonal skills, and must demonstrate commitment as determined by an interview process. To illustrate the level of competition, in 2010, 6,600 applicants competed for 660 available positions in universities.[2] Training encompasses scientific research into teaching and learning, and a practical component that occurs mainly within special teacher training schools that are governed by universities.

New graduates are mentored and teachers have access to continued professional development opportunities throughout their careers. In fact, the school day is structured to enable teachers to pursue professional development, curriculum planning, collaboration, assessment and other related teaching responsibilities within school hours. The successful Finnish model of 'less is more' appears to be a paradox. However, their own research has found little correlation between hours of instruction and resulting student performance. 'The Finnish government understands the importance of teachers and accordingly invests heavily in teacher education and professional development but also work-conducive environments so that the teaching profession attracts and retains talent.'[3] Seymour Sarason (1996) put it succinctly: 'teachers cannot create and sustain contexts for productive learning unless these conditions exist for them'. Needless to say, teacher retention rates in Finland are very good.

Two significant qualities that are linked to the Finnish teaching profession are trust and autonomy. Teachers are regarded as well-educated professionals who are best able to determine the needs of their students and to assess their progress. While guided by the national curriculum, teachers design learning environments to cater for the individual needs of their students. A fundamental difference in the Finnish approach is that 'it is the school, not the system that is the locus of control and capacity'.[4]

Another significant element contributing to Finland's success is the quality and professional leadership of school principals. The same high standard expected of teachers is applied to principals, who are required to have a background with educational, administrative and financial management qualifications.

In Finland, teachers' salaries are incremental, based on experience. 'Paying teachers based on students' test scores or converting public schools to private ones (through charters or other means) are ideas that have no place in the Finnish repertoire for educational improvement.'[5] As Pasi Sahlberg put it, 'Authorities and most parents understand that teaching, caring and educating children is too complex a process to be measured by quantitative metrics alone.'[6]

Teaching methods and approaches

In collaboration with teachers and architects, good ergonomic design is incorporated into Finnish schools because it is recognised that the physical environment is important for learning.

Classes are not streamed in Finnish schools. Since ability grouping was abolished in the 1980s, the achievement gap between high and low achievers began to diminish. In Finland there is a strong belief that all students are capable of achieving, and, to cater for each student, early identification of learning difficulties and the provision of appropriate assistance has raised the standards. Schools have access to teachers trained in special education and also qualified counsellors. No stigma is attached to extra assistance, as assistance is allocated for minor dysfunctions such as speech difficulties or early problems with reading and writing. In fact, 'Almost half of the 16 year olds when they leave comprehensive school, have been engaged in some sort of special education, personalised help or individual guidance.'[7] There is minimal grade repetition as this is considered costly and counterproductive. Early intervention with specifically designed remedial work is far more effective than having a student repeat a grade and be offered the same method that he was unable to master the first time around. As a consequence of these measures, Finland's high standards are evenly distributed across the population.

In Finnish classrooms, there is a strong focus on critical and independent thinking, cooperative learning, creativity and problem-solving. The PISA results highlight how students are able to apply what they have learnt. It is not simply a matter of mastering the curriculum. Finnish schools are able to apply the principle John Dewey advocated, where he 'dreamed of the teacher as a guide helping children formulate questions and devise solutions'.[8] Teachers in Finland are not distracted by external, standardised testing regimes.

Teachers are trusted to know how their students are progressing and they use a diverse variety of assessment tools to monitor their students' progress. Test-based assessment is only part of determining performance. Continuous, diagnostic assessment methods, regular reporting, and national sample-based assessments give clear indications of a student's progress. The only formal examination is the national matriculation exam, which is taken at the end of upper secondary education (age eighteen or nineteen).

Before the first international PISA testing in 2000, countries generally judged and compared their standards on academic competitions, and claimed success on very narrow measurements. For events such as the International Olympiads in subjects such as mathematics, physics and chemistry, only top achievers competed. The other main indicators for comparison were the percentage of a population engaged in tertiary education and the percentage of GDP invested in education.

'The global education reform thinking includes an assumption that competition, choices and more frequent external testing are prerequisites to improving the quality of education.'[9] This trend began with the 1988 Education Reform Act in Margaret Thatcher's England, where test-based accountability and league tables were installed. The model was adopted by other Western nations and eventually spread to Australia. The results speak for themselves. A comparative study of teachers' experiences under different accountability regimes concluded 'the pressure of a structured instructional model of teaching and external assessment of pupils' achievement is having dramatic consequences according to some teachers' (Berry & Sahlberg, 2006). For students, 'Consequences of the high-stakes testing environment include avoidance of risk-taking, boredom and fear.'[10] Evidence indicates Finnish students experience less learning-related anxiety than peers in other countries.

The influence of societal values

An OECD report into Finland's success noted, 'it is hard to imagine how Finland's educational success could be achieved or maintained without reference to the nation's broader and commonly accepted system of distinctive social values that more individualistic and inequitable societies may find it difficult to accept' (Hargreaves et al., 2008).[11]

Shared cultural values translate across all aspects of society. 'Fairness, honesty and social justice are deeply rooted in the Finnish way of life.'[12] Education cannot be seen in isolation. A strong sense of shared responsibility influences policy on health issues, the environment and the economy as well as the education system. Finland also has a strong culture of reading in the home and locals have access to an excellent public library service. The focus on reading reinforces success at the school level.

The value of equality

In Finland, education is regarded as a public good that should be available to all. The vast majority of schools are publically funded and fees are not charged. 'Peruskoulu was built on the social value of equality.'[13] The philosophy of inclusion is seen as the most effective way of accessing and nurturing talent in the community. The practice of early intervention and the provision of support means all students are given the best available opportunities. Within comparable OECD nations, a greater percentage of the population complete higher education and this reform has taken place 'without shifting the burden of cost to students and their parents'.[14]

According to figures from the Human Development Index of the UN (Wilkinson & Pickett), equality provides general benefits to society beyond educational benefits. 'More equitable countries (statistically) have more literate citizens, rarer school drop-out rates, less obesity, better mental health and fewer teenage pregnancies than those where the income gap between poor and wealthy is wider.'[15]

The value of collaboration and cooperation

There are obvious benefits to sharing ideas and successful practices. This is encouraged within the Finnish education system where they recognise that all involved share a common goal. Teachers, parents, unions and local governing bodies share in collaborative networking in the interest of the whole society. A PISA analysis of Finland's success noted, building networks among schools that stimulate and spread innovation helps to explain Finland's success in making 'strong school performance a consistent and predictable outcome throughout the education system' (Schliecher, 2006).[16]

The value of innovation and creativity

Creativity and innovation are nurtured and given priority in Finnish schools. With the focus on teaching rather than testing, Finnish teachers are able to devise programs that challenge children to extend their abilities. While core subjects are thoroughly catered for, other areas of the curriculum are also given priority. As Pasi Sahlberg explains, 'If creativity is defined as coming up with original ideas that have value, then creativity should be as important as literacy and treated with the same status.'[17]

The focus on problem-solving and creative thinking encourages risk-taking and innovation. This approach directly aligns with the needs of industry. To elaborate on this point, a senior member of the Nokia management stated, 'If we hire a youngster who doesn't know all the mathematics or physics that is needed to work here, we have colleagues who can easily teach those things. But if we get somebody who doesn't know how to work with other people, how to think differently or how to create original ideas and somebody who is afraid of making a mistake, there is nothing we can do here. Do what you have to do to keep our education system up-to-date but don't take away creativity and open-mindedness that we now have in our schools.'[18]

The GERM model

The emergence of the Global Education Reform Movement in the 1980s was based on management concepts and principles that are borrowed from the business world. In analysis, this education model is not regarded as a public good but a measurable commodity.

When the principles of competition and accountability are applied to education systems, schools are forced to compete for student resources and are held accountable by means of external, standardised testing and performance indicators.

Pasi Sahlberg has described five common elements of GERM:[19]

Standardisation: using an outcomes-based education program which includes external testing, performance targets, high-stakes accountability and merit-based pay for teachers is an attempt to simplify a complicated issue and offer a quick fix.

Increased focus on core subjects: this involves a narrowing of the curriculum, with literacy and numeracy regarded as the main determinants of perceived success. This comes at the expense of a comprehensive curriculum that would include the arts, social studies and physical education.

Prescribed curriculum: this minimises opportunities for learning methods that encourage experimentation, problem-solving, creativity and risk-taking.

Transfer of models from the corporate world: with a strong influence from private interests, this 'paralyzes teachers' and schools' attempts to learn from the past and learn from each other.'

Adoption of high-stakes, test-based accountability policies: these reward or punish schools and teachers through competition for funding.

Interestingly, this market model is 'often supported by private corporations, consultant firms and private venture philanthropy'.[20] In the business world, their loyalty is to their shareholders and at the same time they advocate a smaller role for government. Perhaps we should scrutinise, or at least query, their motivation.

Fortunately for the Finns, because of the beliefs and practices they developed and adopted, they remained immune from the GERM. Pasi Sahlberg succinctly described how the Finnish way followed 'a professional and democratic path to improvement that grows from the bottom, steers from the top and provides support and pressure from the sides'.[21]

Unfortunately in Australia, we have been swept along with the Anglo/American model, despite the fact that our students have consistently outperformed both the UK and USA in the international PISA testing and assessments since 2000.

I have compiled the table shown on the next two pages to highlight the main points of difference between the Finnish way and the model we have adopted in Australia. I have intentionally simplified the issues in order to highlight the different approaches to the same problem: how to achieve the highest standards of education for our children. The results speak for themselves.

Looking at the chart overleaf, most of the factors that contribute to Finland's successful education system are in stark contrast to the market model adopted by the Australian education system. If we wish to improve our academic achievement, we need to reconsider the direction we have chosen.

The current, successful Finnish model was designed and modified over several decades and the Finns are aware they cannot become complacent about their position. We need to examine our situation, how it evolved and where we need to take it.

In fact, I have often wondered about the structure of our school system in Australia. We began as a group of states in the early days of the colony. Primary education was provided and then secondary education evolved and was added on as such. The particular structure does not appear to have been designed necessarily with educational purposes in mind, but more for ease of administration. When my

Finland	Australia
System-wide	
Education regarded as a public good, a social responsibility and an individual right.	Adoption of the market based model with associated high-stakes testing and accountability.
Publically funded; no fee-charging schools or universities; education seen as a government responsibility.	Increasing trend of privatisation of schools, deregulation of universities and diminishing government support.
Equal opportunity highly valued: equitable results across the country; a socially just system.	Increasing gap between opportunities; expanding academic achievement gap between advantaged and disadvantaged.
Teachers' conditions and pedagogy	
Training: highly competitive, research-based university Master's degree (five to seven years)	Training: Bachelor of Education (four years); university entrance scores vary between states. Additional schemes such as Teach For Australia (graduates given minimal teacher training before being assigned classes).
Teachers are highly valued and respected professionals; excellent teacher retention rates.	Less respect for teachers from society; low morale, growing teacher attrition rate; teacher accountability based on high-stakes, narrow external testing results.
High level of trust for teachers by parents and community.	Less trust; politically driven doubts in teachers' and schools' ability to educate.
Teacher autonomy: time allocated for curriculum development, school improvement, professional development; flexibility to design programs and assessments tailored to individual student's needs.	Increasingly restricted, inflexible, prescriptive, externally directed teaching; demands on accountability and additional administrative loads; professional development mostly in own time and often at own cost.
Teachers' salaries are comparable to other professionals such as doctors and lawyers; incremental with experience.	Teachers' salaries are much lower; moving to teacher performance pay model based on narrow testing results (failed in USA).

Teaching methods and common values

Formal school starting age seven years.	Formal school starting age five years.
Assessment: sample-based continuous assessment by teachers using various assessment techniques; no external standardised testing. Teachers able to focus on individualised teaching using a broad curriculum.	NAPLAN standardised testing attached to high stakes league tables and My School website, as well as regular teacher assessment and reporting. Increasing trend to teaching to the test and narrowing of the curriculum.
Comprehensive curriculum; teachers allowed the flexibility to focus on fostering creativity, problem-solving, innovation, risk-taking, arts and citizenship as well as core academic subjects.	Dominant focus on core subjects at the expense of a broader curriculum (arts, creativity, sports); resulting in student anxiety, risk aversion and boredom.
Cooperation, collaboration, collegiality and networking.	Increasing trend towards competition between schools partly due to high-stakes league tables promoting so-called choice-based on unreliable and incomplete standardised testing.
Fewer face-to-face teaching hours.	More face-to-face teaching hours.
Less homework set.	More homework set.
Less after hours tutoring.	Increasing trend to private, after-hours tutoring.
Teacher-focus on design of individual student development.	Focus on benchmark and standardisation and performance indicators.
Focus on early intervention and special education assistance.	Less funding allocated to early intervention and special education assistance (resulting in more remedial work later).
Support of qualified counsellors.	Less access to qualified counsellors; school chaplain scheme in state schools.

Results

Consistently high level of academic achievement.	Declining levels of academic achievement, albeit still above the OECD average.

children moved from primary to high school, I remember noting that it occurred at a time of upheaval in their lives. They moved from being the 'biggest kid on the block' to the 'smallest fish in a big pond' when they reached puberty; a time when they were going through growth spurts and hormonal changes. At that time, they left a school structure with the security of a single classroom with one teacher, to a series of classes with different teachers, having lost many of their close friends who chose to attend different high schools. We don't appear to have given much thought to the optimal time for creating a fundamental transition in their schooling. Perhaps a better arrangement for children would be to consider early childhood schools, followed by middle year schools, and make the change to senior schools at a more stable time in their lives. After all, confidence levels have a dramatic impact on school performance.

It is not practical to suggest that Australia could transplant the Finnish system, given cultural and economic differences. However, we can benefit from observing and analysing successful policies, approaches and principles, and adopting those that can be applied locally. Fundamentally, the differences between the approaches we have taken and that of the Finns lie in two or three principles. The Finns recognised the connection between a successful education system and a successful economy. Education was seen as a top priority and they made a conscious decision to seriously invest in that field. Understanding the principle that equitable societies are more successful, they placed a high value on equality of opportunity for all students, and promoted the principle of cooperation for the collective good rather than encouraging competition between individuals. They focused on supporting a quality teaching service and chose not to engage in standardised testing or teacher-performance pay.

Australia shares many common societal values with Finland. We have a universal healthcare system that is designed to take care of those in need, although it too is severely lacking in government funding. We have a social welfare system that assists low-income families with housing and an aged care pension system; and we have commitments to assist those with disabilities. We do share a belief that a good education is the basic right of all citizens. However, the gap between the advantaged and disadvantaged is widening. One identifiable difference in our circumstances lies in the role of the state and the method of funding and service delivery.

Finland has a high standard of living. Some claim much of Finland's success is due to the country's demographics. It has a homogenous population, although that is changing due to growing migration to Europe. Finland is a relatively small country and it is often claimed it would be difficult to administer similar policies in large countries such as Australia. However, given that the majority of responsibility for public education resides with the states, such policies could be transferrable.

There is an argument that the PISA results are too narrow an assessment of a public education system, as they are limited to assessing ability in mathematics, science and reading. However, the PISA assessment involves more than a simple test. Fifteen-year-olds participating in PISA testing are selected randomly. There is no specific preparation for the test and a series of questionnaires accompanies testing, which gives a more complete assessment of the quality of education achieved. The level of family support for the student involved, socio-economic background and similar factors are recognised as having a significant impact on the quality of education.

Some claim that as the Finnish language is phonetically based it is much easier for their students to achieve high standards of literacy in their native tongue. Granted, the melting pot that has created the English language, with all its complexities and exceptions to the rules, does result in a greater degree of difficulty for young children to master. Therefore, all the more reason to delay school entry until children have developed the necessary skills and abilities to cope with the unpredictable nature and inconsistencies of the English language. For example, it's an extremely abstract concept for young children to understand that the phoneme 'ou' sounds different in the words could, sound, enough, through, though and thought.

If policy-makers seriously adopted an evidence-based approach to examining the elements of successful education systems, the comparisons and contrasts between what we have adopted and what actually delivers success would be obvious. The benefits of an excellent education system naturally flow on to the workforce. A recent World Economic Forum Report identified Finland as 'the world's most competitive economy'.[22] In addition, Finland is recognised by Forbes as one of the happiest countries in the world.[23] We could learn a lot from them. It's worth a look!

7

Conclusion

> 'One generation plants the trees, and another gets the shade.'
> – Chinese proverb

In recent years, the focus on commodifying education services has diverted attention away from the fundamental purpose of education in society. Education is a universal right and an investment in the future. Funding of this basic service has been the subject of much debate and the duplication of state and federal systems of government has led to redundancies and an ineffective delivery of service. Too much importance has been attached to metrics, such as the narrow and misleading NAPLAN testing and associated My Schools website, the resulting league tables and the planned teacher performance pay system. If Australia is to regain its status as one of the top performing OECD countries, we need to examine the models implemented by successful education systems and adopt and adapt those methods. We need to reassess our approach to funding and embrace the recommendations outlined in the Gonski funding reforms.

The market model

The recent trend in public discourse with frequent reference to economies rather than societies reflects the changing bias and values that are influencing Western nations.

We need to clarify the distinctions between how the private sector operates and how public services are delivered. The private sector operates on a narrow range of measurable performance indicators. The ultimate focus is on profits that will please investors.

Public goods and services such as education do not operate on those principles, mainly because they are provided in response to market failures, and their benefits provide for society as a whole. They are therefore appropriately funded by the taxpayer. Public education has become embroiled in a business model that is inappropriate and based on weak and contestable economic argument.

So who is promoting this agenda? Pasi Sahlberg revealed that the GERM movement has been promoted by 'international development agencies, bilateral donors and private consultants through their interventions in national education reforms and policy making processes'.[1] He quotes Diane Ravitch, historian of American education, who describes 'how venture philanthropy injects billions of dollars into public education systems in the US' (and other countries), 'and often insists on employing management concepts and principles borrowed from the business world in the school system' (Ravitch 2010). Such concepts do not transfer successfully to education programs.

The market model as applied to public education is not economically driven but ideologically driven. The conservative push towards 'small government' demands privatisation of services to ease fiscal pressure on government spending. If we left everything to the free market, there would be no role left for government. Unfettered market forces would lead to anarchy. However, not even extreme proponents of the free market argue for the total elimination of government. The issue is therefore one of balance. How much free market will work and how much government intervention is enough? Experiments in pushing the limit have yielded unconvincing evidence for the pro-market advocates.

We already have the example of how the free market affects the private health system in America, whereby unfortunate families have been bankrupted by ill-health. President Obama has faced fierce opposition from the conservatives in the Tea Party in his efforts to make healthcare in the US affordable and available to all.

Privatising the water supply too could lead to dire consequences if left open to exploitation or sabotage. Yet this very proposal was actually expressed by Peter Brabeck, former CEO of Nestlé in an interview for a documentary called *We Feed the World*.[2] His view was, 'Water is a foodstuff like any other and it should have a market value.'

Coincidentally, Nestlé controls a large percentage of the bottled water industry.

I could go on. Already much of the world's food supply is under the control of multinational corporations, the biggest of which is Monsanto. These corporations are utilising intellectual property laws in an attempt to control seed production, and are bullying governments into substandard food-labelling laws. Factory-farming methods are putting profit ahead of animal welfare and consumer health. It seems the world's resources, once freely enjoyed by us all, have become commodities.

Early colonial powers were able to achieve economic gains through exploitation of slave labour, not through their own innovation, creativity or personal endeavour. The same principle of exploiting others continues today with corporations profiting from sweatshops in Asian countries. I once asked a banker, 'How much is enough? At what point would banks be satisfied with their level of profit?' After some thoughtful consideration, his response was 'Never.' So where does it end?

What is the agenda behind privatising everything? Basically it allows those with wealth and power to reduce complex markets to simplistic questions of supply, demand and price, while failing to address the subtle realities of the value to society of outcomes that are difficult, if not impossible to quantify. Raj Patel, in his book *The Value of Nothing*, clarifies the issue.

> Education and health are goods that have a higher social benefit than the individual private benefit to the person who receives them. In the economic literature there's a class of goods that not only have a higher social than private benefit, but which by their very nature need nonmarket means to provide them; these are called public goods.[3]

In fact, society values primary education so highly it is classified as mandatory.

Unfortunately, when the mantra is to succeed no matter what, and when profit is the only motivation, ethics are often compromised or even abandoned. This has been revealed by several recent public enquiries into donations to political parties in return for favours or preferential treatment. Issues of public good or collective responsibility are subordinated to rent-seeking behaviour. Private monopolies of any sort, but particularly those involving media control, threaten democracy.

Reawin Connell of the University of Sydney candidly expresses it this way

> Markets commodify things – that is basic. If you ration education, you can sell a privilege to those with enough advantage and you can reduce the need for public investment in education for all. That's what the market agenda in education basically does.[4]

Joel Klein, the source of inspiration for our very own NAPLAN, and former New York City schools chancellor, went on to work for Rupert Murdoch as a senior adviser 'on a wide range of initiatives, including developing business strategies for the emerging education marketplace'.[5] Klein noted that spending on US education doubled over the period from 1970 to 2008, yet it was not matched by improvements in students' performance. He commented that if the education system was a business, 'It would have been shut down a long time ago.' Perhaps instead of regarding it in market terms he should re-examine the effectiveness of the programs that were initiated and conclude that the system needs to reconsider the approaches that were adopted, including his own initiative in the New York district.[6]

It was revealed in 2010 'that the improvements (in student results in the New York district) were a sham, being driven by lower pass standards'.[7] In addition, Klein's '$75m teacher performance pay scheme, which he described as "transcendent" when introduced in 2007, was also a stunning failure'. A study published by Harvard University economist Roland Fryer found that 'it failed to increase student achievement', and the incentive scheme 'was quietly abandoned last year'.

Undeterred, Klein believed that the 'huge transformation in the field of education that is coming is going to be driven by private markets'.[8] Murdoch identified 'a multibillion dollar opportunity in the education sector, and followed up on the goal of capitalizing on that market share by buying Wireless Generation and launching Amplify'.[9] News Corporation's education unit, Amplify, worth one hundred million dollars annually, developed digitised textbooks and created its own tablets for use in classrooms. In response, the US based research group the Pew Internet Research Centre has warned that 'the gulf between children with access to smartphones and tablets, and those without is getting larger', and so the opportunity gap will widen.[10] This trend in Western society has led to inequities in opportunity and ultimately is detrimental to society as a whole.

In 2015, News Corp was preparing to sell its digital education business. Early technical difficulties and competition from established education giants such as Pearson and McGraw-Hill resulted in reduced profits. However, Klein determined that the company would explore 'strategic alternatives' and focus its efforts 'on the growth and success of our digital curriculum and assessment products'.

If education is to be viewed as a commodity, measured and sold for profit, then free-market forces will ensure there is a greater divide between the haves and the have-nots. Instead of an equitable service well-funded by taxes and wisely administered with checks and balances, governments would be allowed to abandon their social responsibilities, and hand the future of education to commercial interests. Private companies sponsoring schools would have control over how schools were administered and the contents of their curriculum.

In her book *The Death and Life of the Great American School System*, Diane Ravitch reveals that after examining the evidence, she changed her mind about the best direction for public education, and demonstrates that methods such as choice and testing simply did not work. They have failed to deliver. Ravitch is concerned that 'how much you earn has a great deal to do with where you were educated'. Conservatives have traditionally opposed government involvement and influence in education and advocate deregulation. Yet, as she points out, 'it was the unregulated, free-market model of competition and choice that ultimately led to the great financial collapse in 2008'.[11] Ironically, those companies had to be bailed out by governments, and unfortunately not a lot appears to have been learnt from the experience.

Clearly there is an essential role for government in many services, and education and health are two that have a direct impact on families and the economy.

Investing in education

To the extent that education can be viewed in economic terms, it should be seen as an investment, not a cost. And this is where governments experience difficulties. By its very nature, the evaluation of education programs is a long term project. Australian governments have short, three-year terms in which to prove their effectiveness. Traditionally, they have been reluctant to invest in long-term projects, preferring instead highly visible undertakings such as schools building programs.

Arguments over funding arise largely because of the division of responsibility for education between federal and state governments. This dysfunctional arrangement has resulted in inefficient duplication of services and has enabled both parties opportunities to absolve themselves of responsibility when problems are identified. The blame game is also practised in health services, where states are responsible for hospitals while the federal government is responsible for medical research.

The funding model used for the last decade has led to inequities in educational opportunities. The Gonski report identified a widening gap between the performances of students from lower economic status backgrounds compared to those from more privileged sections of our society. If we want a productive, effective economy, we need to invest in an educated population. When tertiary education is only readily available to those from a more privileged background, then society as a whole is disadvantaged, because we are not benefiting from the potential talent, skills and ability of a much wider range within the community. If we design an education system that delivers a well-educated population, the whole of the nation ultimately benefits with increased productivity and a workforce that is better equipped to compete in world markets.

> 'There is only one thing that costs more than education today: the lack of it.' – Anonymous

The funding issue

If we value excellence in education, then we need to fund it adequately through the tax system. Taxation, however, has become a dirty word in Australian politics. Politicians have become mesmerised by running budget surpluses. They are reluctant to increase direct taxes and in most elections have promised to cut taxes. Governments would also prefer to cut public services rather than address the problem of declining revenue. Australians have become accustomed to this and now routinely demand increasingly better services without paying for them. To an extent, it might seem unfair to blame politicians for underfunded services while we, the public, demand tax cuts. But part of good public governance is to shift attitudes when necessary. We need to reassess how services should be funded.

There are no quick fixes. Glib slogans do not deliver results. There is no simple formula with isolated solutions. As outlined by Pasi Sahlberg,

> Finland is said to have well-prepared teachers, pedagogically designed schools, good school principals, a relatively homogenous society, an inclusive national education vision, and emphasis on special needs – each separately and collectively help the Finnish education system to perform well.[12]

For the Finns, it took several decades and determined research and investment to develop a world-class education system. Interestingly, cost alone is not the answer either. It has been found that the level of expenditure is not directly related to results and does not guarantee success. Finland actually invests less than the OECD average. According to 2009 figures, the total public expenditure on education, as a percentage of GDP, was 5.6% in 2007 while the OECD average was 5.7% (and the US average was 6%).[13] Yet Finland has been able to provide an excellent education at a reasonable cost because they took into account the longer-term consequences and invested wisely.

As an example that demonstrates how money is invested wisely and how money is saved, Finland's policy of early identification of learning difficulties, and the provision of expert special education assistance to help overcome those problems, means the majority of students are able to achieve a high standard and there is less need for remedial work. 'Finnish experience and international research shows that investment in early childhood development pays off in later grades through better aptitude and learning skills, and positive outcomes.'[14] Similarly the Finnish policy of not repeating classes, in addition to avoiding the social stigma attached, avoids the costs and inadequacies associated with this practice.

Spending taxpayer's money is clearly a complex issue both economically and politically. Spending is subject to competing priorities and governments are accountable sooner or later for the wisdom or folly for the choices they make. In Australia, according to economist Andrew Charlton, 'As the [mining] boom took off between 2004 and 2007, it added $334 billion in windfall gains to the budget. Australia saved only 6% of this, using the remaining 94% to fund tax cuts and spending increases.'[15] The Howard–Costello government proudly boasted a string of budget surpluses while downplaying growing concerns about underinvesting in services, infrastructure and skills. Worse, their popular and unsustainable tax cuts were 'heavily skewed to high income earners.'[16] Of course, once taxes are reduced, it is unpalatable for succeeding governments to reverse the situation and propose tax increases. Over time, this has significantly reduced the government's ability to generate income, leaving us with a funding problem for education.

Taxes are a social responsibility and under Australia's progressive tax system those who can afford more should contribute more. Mining resources are finite and they belong to the Australian population, both now and to future generations. The proposed mineral resource rent tax was a fairer way to collect the economic rent for Australia's minerals boom and provide vital funding for community services, such as education. Subsidising mining companies is illogical, particularly when, according to Paul Cleary in his book *Too Much Luck*, a large percentage of profits are going out of Australia and, in fact 'overall foreign ownership of mining is at more than 80%'.[17]

In the 1970s, Ross Garnaut and Anthony Clunnes-Ross helped devise a resource rental tax (PRT) 'that would capture a fair share of profits without undermining investment in the [petroleum] industry'.[18] When the Hawke government announced their intention to introduce the PRT for the offshore petroleum industry, there was an outcry from the opposition and a campaign of scare mongering claiming it would deter investment. They were proved wrong. The introduction of the PRT was followed by substantial investment in offshore gas petroleum.

Bob Brown, former Greens leader, suggested we should have created a sovereign wealth fund from our mining wealth. Norway funds their excellent education system this way, and they have preserved savings for future generations by setting up a sovereign fund to protect the nation for when the resources windfall ends.

So what of the future? We need to look ahead and consider funding sources when Chinese demand for our resources diminishes. The mining boom saw the contraction of our manufacturing sector therefore we need to anticipate future markets. We need to be flexible and consider diversifying our production of goods and services to enable us to adjust to changing economic circumstances.

Global climate change is a growing concern, and investment in alternative energy sources is inevitable. We have a choice. The demand for fossil fuels, a finite resource, is unsustainable. Australia has the opportunity to become a leader. We can view investment in renewable energies as an economic opportunity or we can be left behind. Australia is blessed with more hours of sunlight than many countries in the northern hemisphere, yet nations like Germany have taken the lead in solar energy production. We also have opportunities to invest in geothermal energy production, an emission-free energy that is extracted from the earth's natural, stored heat. Wind power also can produce electricity that replaces power that would otherwise be generated by burning fossil fuels. All of these alternative energy sources would reduce exposure of the economy to fuel price volatility, at the same time offering environmentally friendly alternatives. Now is not the time to ignore the issue of climate change and abandon all meaningful measures that tackle it. We need to encourage innovation and research. In Australia we have no shortage of innovative and creative thinkers, many of whom we lose to the brain drain overseas. Now is not the time to be slashing funding to research organisations such as the CSIRO. Neither is it a wise move for a government to neglect to include a dedicated science minister in its cabinet. Now is not the time to be reducing funding to education and deregulating universities. We should be investing in a strong education system for future generations. We need to be looking forward, not backwards, or we will be left behind.

Addressing the problem of funding is always going to be a contentious issue, as is spending priorities. I remember with affection the tea towel that declared, 'I long for the day when defence forces are rattling cans and running raffles and cake stalls to raise the money for their toys'. Governments are commonly influenced by powerful lobby groups, but they should also be listening to the families who voted for them and who value education and health as the most important essential services.

The Gonski funding model

The Gonski Review consisted of a panel of experts headed by businessman, Professor David Gonski. The review was established in 2010 to examine school funding in Australia and determine changes necessary to improve the quality and equity of our school system. It found that Australia has been investing too little in education, particularly in public schools, and student performance overall has been declining due to lack of resources. As well, it identified growing performance gaps between students excelling and those struggling. There was in fact a direct correlation between educational outcomes and socio-economic status.

The reforms recommended a system that better targeted funding to meet students' needs. This was to be invested in ways that have been proven to help student needs, including the provision of smaller class sizes, extra specialist teachers in literacy and numeracy, more support for high-need students such as those with disabilities, and additional training and classroom support for teachers.[19]

An OECD study in 2009 reported,

> Longer term investment in education and human capital plays an important role in maximizing productivity. Investments in education and training have multiplier affects that contribute to further innovation and growth.[20]

To date, the total expenditure on education in Australia is well below the OECD average. In 2011, Australia spent 5.2% of gross domestic product (GDP) on education, compared with the average of 5.9% of GDP. This places Australia equal sixth lowest of thirty-one countries.[21] While spending alone does not guarantee a successful system, making education a priority and making wise choices on spending measures does.

The time for change has come. The cost of inaction is immeasurable. The report shows,

> We can't go back from here: the problems are deep and structural and are not only creating division and inequity, but the resulting underachievement is starting to cost the nation.[22]

While there is popular support for the Gonski recommendations, we need to heed the report's warning that

> Unless governments are prepared to step up to the mark and make the necessary investment and other reforms, and unless education sectors can overlook their differences and act cohesively for the good of all students, Australia's schooling system will continue to drift and we will fall further behind the rest of the world.[23]

Unfortunately at present there is no guarantee or commitment to follow this needs-based sector-free program. Funding is only guaranteed for the first four years by the current government, while the majority of the funding is designed to be committed during the following two years.

I don't doubt many politicians have altruistic motives and are genuinely passionate about creating the best education system possible. However, they do need to acknowledge that we should reassess our situation and change direction. We need to move away from the market-driven model with a focus on standardised testing; and politicians need to be guided by professionals in the field who know what methods are effective for learning, and what methods are detrimental to learning. They need to listen, accept professional advice and act on that advice.

A wise choice would be to compare and assess our current position, and then examine successful education systems around the world and decide which elements might be successfully adopted here.

Current education standards

Australian education standards, compared with the rest of the world, have slipped during recent years. In the Program for International Student Assessment (PISA) test in 2003, of the thirty participating OECD countries, Australia was ranked fourth in reading skills, eighth in maths and fifth in science. In 2009, with sixty-two countries participating, we were ranked ninth in reading, fifteenth in maths and tenth in science.[24] In fairness, as more nations joined in PISA testing, there was a much larger field competing, so to presume our ranking has slipped due only to falling standards is not entirely true. The comparisons are between a different set of participants. Nevertheless, we should note that Australia still performs at levels 'significantly above' the OECD average in mathematics, science and reading skills.[25]

Recently, Australia also participated in two other international tests: Trends in International Mathematics and Science Study (TIMSS) and Progress in International Reading and Literacy Study (PIRLS). These tested reading, writing and mathematics for Years 4 and 8. Of the forty-eight countries that participated, Australia was ranked twenty-seventh.

It is intriguing why we in Australia consistently appear to adopt systems that have failed elsewhere. Australian students have consistently performed at a higher level than those in UK and USA. Why then do we look to them for inspiration? We have close cultural ties and there are many qualities to admire about both nations, but the direction of their education systems is not one we should be following.

Christopher Bantick, an education commentator and senior literature teacher at a Melbourne Anglican boys independent school, was teaching in England when the Thatcher government introduced league tables. He came to the conclusion that 'Australia is beginning to mirror exactly the problems that have beset British schooling.'[26] Robert Crosby, a Labour Party member in the UK, has also commented on the market-driven, autonomous approach to education. He noted that since the Conservative government came to power, 'public amenities, including our schools are under attack. Private profit-seekers sit waiting like vultures to pick over our services for their own gain.'[27] He noted, 'conservative politicians in the UK have made concerted attempts to undermine and de-stabilize state schools over decades'. Michael Gove, the former Education Secretary, set up largely autonomous academies that 'do not have to follow the National Curriculum; they are being encouraged to employ non-qualified teachers and there have already been examples of financial impropriety in some academies'. If this is the case, it is not a path we should be following.

If we choose to make comparisons via league tables, let's take a closer look at the PISA results. Note that the PISA organisation is not interested or concerned with test results alone. PISA analysis refers to scores along with responses to surveys which are designed to assess the degree of influence and support from home backgrounds. It also indicates how students use their knowledge and it assesses students' thinking skills. The purpose of PISA testing is not to rank countries competitively. Their main concern is to encourage participating countries to use the findings to improve their own teaching and student performance. Conclusions from PISA analysis indicate that the amount of money countries allocate for education is not as important as how and where it is directed.

As a matter of interest and general observation, PISA results found differences in gender performance. Generally, girls outperform boys in reading, boys outperform girls in mathematics, and there is no noticeable difference in science results.

The first PISA test programs included only thirty countries. In 2012, there were sixty-five participating countries, including thirty-four from the OECD group and thirty-one partner countries.

I have already extensively discussed the merits of the system used in Finland. Notably, several Asian countries are also performing extremely well. When deciding which programs could be successfully adopted in Australia, we need to examine not only results but methods practised and cultural influences. Singapore and Hong Kong, for instance, hold different cultural values. Parents in Singapore have high expectations and are very ambitious for their children's success. They have a respect for learning and for authority and the society is disciplined and focused. However, success often comes at a social cost. Students in some Asian countries commonly live with high levels of stress, depression and myopia (near-sightedness). The extensive culture of tutoring and coaching outside of school hours does not only contribute to pressure and anxiety, but it is an inefficient method of improving standards. Until recently in South Korea, children attended school six days a week. Education professor Yong Zhao has noted the PISA 2009 did not receive much attention in the Chinese media, and that the high scores in China are due to excessive workload and testing, adding that it's 'no news that the Chinese education system is excellent in preparing outstanding test-takers, just like other education systems within the Confucian cultural circle; Singapore, Korea, Japan and Hong Kong'.[28] More recently, however, another analysis noted a 'sea change in pedagogy' in the highly successful Shanghai education system. They

> abandoned their focus on educating a small elite, and instead worked to construct a more inclusive system. They also significantly increased teacher's pay and training, reducing the emphasis on rote learning and focusing classroom activities on problem solving.[29]

So which top-performing education systems have policies that could be successfully adopted by Australia? Having discussed the difficulty we already experience in achieving a work-life balance in Australia, I would not advocate accelerating stress levels. Given the academic success and equality of the Finnish model, and noting other societal values that have been measured, including general levels of well-being and happiness, I would favour adopting a system more like the Finnish education system.

Elements of success from high-achieving countries

Expert analysis of PISA results has revealed a profile of common elements of successful education systems. A major influence is equality. 'High performing school systems tend to allocate resources more equitably across socio economically advantaged and disadvantaged schools.'[30] As well,

> Top performers place great emphasis on selecting and training teachers, encourage them to work together and prioritise investment in teacher quality. They also set clear targets and give teachers autonomy in the classroom to achieve them.' In Finland and Singapore investment is

directed to pre-service and beginning teachers. Access to professional development, and collaboration and mentoring programs with senior teachers ensure continual learning and development.[31]

Equality

In 2012, the OECD released a report 'acknowledging that gaining inequality was undermining economic growth', and 'inequality in opportunities and earnings will affect economic performance as a whole'.[32]

So let's look at some of those issues in detail. In his book *Battlers and Billionaires: The Story of Inequality in Australia*, Andrew Leigh, Australian politician and former economics professor at the ANU, noted that Australia has the ninth highest level of inequality among thirty-four rich countries.[33] Levels of inequality have risen since the 1980s due to several factors. Globalisation, a reduction in union membership and tax cuts for the wealthy have contributed to this. The Gonski Review identified a widening gap between the achievement of advantaged and disadvantaged students in Australia, at the same time as our average results were declining. As we are increasingly influenced by the market model, it is helpful to examine how that model affects the issue of equality.

Journalist and commentator Waleed Ali, in his *Quarterly Essay* 'What's Right? The Future of Conservativism in Australia', made an interesting observation. He described markets as amoral. 'They only have one necessary value – efficiency.'[34] He noted that neo-liberalism 'is quite comfortable with unequal income distributions'. When the Treasurer delivers a budget where cuts fall disproportionately on lower-income families, thus further widening the disparity between the wealthy and the poor, and then declares, 'Striving to achieve equality is not the role of government', the ideology upon which he bases his decisions is obvious; and he clearly does not understand the principle that equitable societies are more successful.[35]

Admittedly, it is easier to achieve opportunities for all in a homogenous society. But in Australia we live in a multicultural society with a large proportion of students having English as a second language. As well, our indigenous population represents a disproportionate percentage of low academic achievers. Apart from the ethical issue of the basic right for each child to be provided with a quality education; if we were to focus on the provision of special education support and resources for those who are in most need, then we would raise the nation's average results at the same time. In market model terms, this is an investment in human capital. Regrettably, in recent years successful programs such as Reading Recovery and English as a second language (ESL) support have been abandoned, not because they were ineffective but because of the cost of the programs. This has been proven to be short-sighted and costly in the long term as standards are perceived to have slipped.

Teachers and pedagogy

Nations with the highest levels of academic success recognise teachers as pivotal to their success. They invest in training and ongoing professional support. Teachers in these societies are respected, valued and trusted, and remuneration levels are comparable to other highly qualified professions. To ensure continued success, Pasi Sahlberg has noted,

> A critical condition for attracting the most able young people year after year to teacher education is that a teacher's work should represent an independent and respectful profession rather than merely focus on technical implementation of externally mandated standards, endless tests and administrative burdens.[36]

In societies with successful education systems, parents and the community support teachers and work together, recognising their common goals and striving together for optimum outcomes for the next generation.

The common values and pedagogical elements of successful education systems include
- promoting identification of learning difficulties, and early intervention supported by special education-trained teachers and qualified counsellors;
- avoiding early tracking that directs students towards a choice of academic or vocational paths; avoiding ability grouping and the practice of repeating;

- developing a broad, comprehensive curriculum which embraces the Arts as well as proficiency in literacy and numeracy;
- allowing for the flexibility and autonomy of a teaching style that enables teachers to focus on and encourage creativity, innovation, problem-solving, risk-taking and inter-personal skill development; and
- embracing the philosophy of cooperation and collaboration rather than competition.

In other words, the focus is not so much on content as method. What is taught is not as important as how it is taught, with the focus on teaching students how to apply their skills and knowledge.

Assessment

The other common element of successful education systems lies in their assessment methods. These systems do not employ external, standardised testing programs. Teachers are trusted to know their student's progress and are encouraged to engage in a wide variety of continual assessment methods in addition to authentic, individualised testing.

As a clear indication of the dissatisfaction teachers feel about the ineffective practice of over-testing, a recent letter from a teacher to her pupils following their public exam results received overwhelming support when it went viral on Twitter in August 2014. The head teacher at Barrowford Primary School in Lancashiire, Rachel Tomlinson, told her students,

> The people who create these tests and score them do not know each of you – the way your teachers do, the way I hope to, and certainly not the way your families do. They do not know that many of you speak two languages. They do not know that you can play a musical instrument or that you can dance or paint a picture. They do not know that your friends count on you to be there for them or that your laughter can brighten the dreariest day.

The letter was modelled on a research paper written by an American teacher and academic, Kimberly A. Hurd, and the sentiment very clearly resonated with teachers around the world.[37]

In Australia, the AEU has called for an overhaul of the NAPLAN testing regime. Former president Angelo Gavrielatos suggested, 'Let's re-examine the purpose and administration because, in its current form, with the associated high stakes, it is being counterproductive and indeed, damaging in many regards.'[38] As a suggestion for an improved model, it has been proposed that the Literacy and Numeracy NAPLAN tests be taken online by 2016. This would speed up the time it takes students to receive results and could become a genuine diagnostic tool without some of the problems currently associated with NAPLAN. A new model could be tailored to fit the ability of each child, with those answering several questions correctly being given more advanced questions until they reach the true limit of their ability, thus revealing their full potential; and those struggling could be offered less demanding options.

Or perhaps we should consider an alternative national assessment, more along the lines of the PISA testing program, which would provide a national snapshot with a more realistic assessment of level of understanding, achievement and application of skills. With this model, randomly selected candidates are given tests designed to assess their application of skills and knowledge. The emphasis is not on the testing alone. There is no downtime for preparation and therefore no distortion of teaching methods, narrowing of the curriculum or attachment to high stakes. The assessment is more comprehensive because it is accompanied by surveys assessing family and background influence and level of support. Analysis of a system-wide program such as this would provide valuable feedback on student achievement on a national level. This would enhance the regular, comprehensive reporting and detailed feedback that is currently provided on an individual basis by teachers in Australian schools.

> 'The direction in which education starts a man will determine his future life.' – Plato

The present and the future

My message to parents is, do not succumb to scaremongering about the standards of our teachers and schools. You can trust our teachers to have a thorough understanding of how children learn. The vast majority are dedicated, competent professionals who invest more of their energy and time than is sometimes understood, appreciated or even expected. If you need reassurance, go down to your local school and ask questions, observe, get involved and see for yourself.

You can have faith in your children's potential. With their natural abilities, their curiosity and their drive to learn, given the right conditions they will not only survive, they will thrive.

The pervading pessimism in our society is unfounded. It is driven by political forces. Australia survived the Global Financial Crisis remarkably well. It was the only major developed nation to avoid the 2009 worldwide recession. With a AAA credit rating, we have more favourable economic conditions than most other developed nations. There is no 'budget emergency' in Australia. Our unemployment levels are low (5.5% in April 2013 compared to 12.1% in the euro zone);[39] and 6.3% as of July 2015.[40] Inflation is low and our 'gross government debt remains low at 35% which is about one third of the OECD average'.[41] Current low interest rates are assisting those with mortgages and also housing market investors. In fact,

> In 2013 the World Bank published its World Development Indicators, which showed that Australia had risen to be the seventh-richest nation in the world, our highest position in more than a hundred years.[42]

We live in a safe country. We are not traumatised by civil wars or abject poverty. Our environment is not polluted and we take it for granted that we are able to breathe clean air. Contrary to the popular myth, we are not being invaded by hordes of asylum seekers. Australia's asylum seeker numbers, while politically sensitive, remain numerically small. Of the 43.7 million people displaced in 2010, Australia hosted 0.2% of the world's refugees.[43] To put it in perspective, in 2012 Australia received 8,250 asylum claims via air and sea arrivals. In the same period, the US received 55,500, France 47,800 and Germany 41,300. In fact, 80% of the world's refugees are hosted in the developing world, with Pakistan hosting the largest number of refugees worldwide.[44] During 2013, numbers escalated, perhaps in response to events worldwide rather than as a direct result of Australian policy on refugees.

During 2014 and 2015, the refugee crisis in Europe dramatically escalated and has become the largest migration of asylum seekers since World War II. It has seen desperate refugees fleeing war and persecution in Syria, North Africa and Afghanistan. Germany alone is expecting 800,000 refugees to arrive throughout 2015. Such figures demonstrate the magnitude of the problem worldwide and, at the same time, starkly contrast with the impact on Australia. In fact, there is a humanitarian case for Australia to share more of the burden rather than spend millions of dollars on 'border protection' designed to 'keep people out'.

In 2013 an exhibition at the Australian National Museum, titled Glorious Days, highlighted life in Australia one hundred years ago. It celebrated 'the vibrancy of Australia in 1913, when people optimistically embraced the modern world and all it offered'. So what has happened to our optimism in recent years? Why are we so anxious? Perhaps we have become more self-centred, or have we been conditioned to believe we deserve more?

As journalist and economics commentator Matt Wade observed, 'You might have missed it but Australia recently got some excellent news. The United Nations declared Australia at the vanguard of human progress.'[45] Australia ranked second to Norway on the UN's human development index, which ranks countries according to wealth and investment in population. This takes into account health and education and several other key measures of well-being such as life expectancy. The UN estimates Australia's 'gross national income per capita increased by about 77% between 1980 and 2012'.

So instead of talking down the economy, and talking down our teachers and their valuable contribution to the education system, our government and policy-makers need to take a look at what's really happening, and make a genuine effort to take every measure possible to ensure a successful future for the next generation. They need to recognise the link between an equitable and successful education system and a successful economy. They need to make education a priority. They need to abandon failed ideologies and make decisions based on facts; assess elements of successful education systems and adopt policies that will improve student academic achievement.

Ultimately, we have to decide what we want for our children's future. Do we want a cohesive and equitable society that values our universal healthcare system, caters for disability services and supports and promotes education as a public good and a right? Do we still value a fair go for all? What sort of workforce will be created from our education system? Do we want mediocrity and conformity or do we want creative, confident, innovative, independent thinkers? After all, these children will be the scientists and inventors and leaders of the future. Given the best tools, they may discover clever and affordable ways to use renewable energy sources to service the energy needs of the future. They may develop systems to protect the world's environment and, with the right support and encouragement, they will achieve the skills and abilities to secure a successful and vibrant society.

> Teachers are verbal by nature. They are observers by profession. They spend all day with the most important commodity in the world, our children.' – Catherine Collins and Douglas Frantz

Notes

1

1. Wu, Margaret, The Misuse of NAPLAN Data, www.nswtf.org.au, September 2010
2. *Fighting For Equality In Education*, Save Our Schools, 17 January 2012
3. Hornsby, David & Lorraine Wilson, *Teaching To the Test*
4. ibid.
5. The Experience of Education: the impact of high-stakes testing on school students and their families. Survey carried out by the University of Melbourne, commissioned by the Whitlam Institute, 2012
6. www.abc.net.au/news, 26 November 2012
7. Mulheron, Maurie www.canberra.times.com.au/opinion/political-news/naplan, 19 June 2013
8. Bonner, Chris & Jane Caro, *The Stupid Country*, p. 61
9. Wilcox, Cathy, *Canberra Times*, 6 May 2013
10. Simons, John, article by Bernard Lane, *The Australian*, 17 May 2011
11. Caldwell, Brian, article by Paul Osborne, *The Australian*, 1 November 2010
12. Cobold, Trevor, 'Save Our Schools', *Canberra Times*, 26 May 2013
13. Australian Education Union, Senate Committee Report, Education, Employment and Workforce Relations Reference Committee, November 2010
14. Wu, Margaret, op. cit.
15. Bonnor, Chris & Jane Caro, op. cit., p. 165
16. Performance Pay: The Research, AEU Victorian Branch Submission, www.performanceincentives.org/data/files, June 2012
17. National Bureau of Economic Research, Save Our Schools, August 2010 and July 2011
18. Ravitch, Diane, *The Death and Life of the Great American School System*, SOS, August 2010
19. www.saveourschools.com.au, 12 August 2010
20. Masters, Geoff, 'School Improvement', ACER Research Developments No. 28, Summer 2012
21. SOS Education Brief, 2010
22. The Hechinger Report, www.saveourschools.com.au, 23 September 2010
23. The Experience of Education: The Impact of High-Stakes Testing on Students and Their Families, www.abc.net.org/news, 26 November 2012

24. http://education.nswtf.org.au/june-02-2014/news-4-naplan-failed-reform

2

1. Copink, Alison, Patricia Kuhl & Andrew Meltzoff, *The Scientist in the Crib*, p. 1
2. Ibid., p. 28
3. Ibid., p. 25
4. Ibid., p. 94
5. Ibid., p. 153
6. Ibid., p. 100
7. Doidge, Norman, *The Brain That Changes Itself*, p. 15
8. Ibid., p. 51
9. Ibid., p. 52
10. Sheridan, Mary, *Play In Early Childhood*
11. 'The Arts and Australian Education: Realising Potential', *Australian Education Review*, No. 58
12. Robinson, Ken, *The Element: How Finding Your Passion Changes Everything*
13. Gill, Richard, *National Times*, 9 February 2011
14. Hornsby, David & Lorraine Wilson, op. cit.
15. www.movetolearn.com.au
16. Siegel, Daniel, *Mindsight: Change Your Brain and Your Life*, p. 84
17. Pheloung, Barbara, *Overcoming Learning Difficulties*, p. 75
18. Ibid.
19. Biddulph, Steve, *Raising Boys*
20. Siegel, Dan, op. cit., p. 108
21. Ibid., p. 108
22. Ibid., p. 41
23. Ibid., p. 40
24. Doidge, Norman, op. cit. p. 139
25. Kennedy, Gerry; 'Facing Challenges of Learning'; *Canberra Times*, 11 February 2012

3

1. Walker, Kathy, *The Walker Learning Approach Years 3–8*
2. Forest Kindergartens, Wikipedia.org.wiki/Forest_kindergartens
3. Pheloung, Barbara, *School Floors*, p. 212
4. Ibid. p. 221
5. Anderson, Professor Warwick, CEO, National Health and Medical Research Council (NHMRC), 2009
6. NSW Government Health, September 2007
7. www.movetolearn.com.au
8. Hannaford, Carla, *Smart Moves*
9. www.thelisteningprogram.com
10. Doidge, Norman, op. cit.
11. Kavli Foundation Announcement 2 April, 2013
12. Doidge, Norman, op. cit. p. 70
13. Doidge, Norman, op. cit. p. 72
14. Doidge, Norman, op. cit. p. 88

4

1. Abuelaish, Izzeldin, *I Shall Not Hate*, p. 42
2. Ibid., p. 45
3. A Snapshot of Schools in Australia 2013, McCrindle Research and Australian Social Trends; Bureau of Statistics 2008
4. www.smh.com.au/opinion/blogs/learning-curve/is-australia-on-the-right-path
5. www.smh.com.au, October 2012

6. Press Club presentation, 2012
7. Goleman, Daniel, *Social Intelligence*, p. 86
8. www.badapplebullies.com/research.htm
9. Beth Osborne, *Oprah*, November 2011
10. Adoniou, Misty, *Canberra Times*, 17 December 2013
11. Sahlberg, Pasi, *Finnish Lessons*, p. 94
12. *Courier Mail*, 17 November 2012
13. *Canberra Times*, 14 April 2013
14. www.bbc.co.uk, 25 March 2013
15. AEU *Public Education Voice*, June 2012
16. www.badapplebullies.com/research
17. *Sydney Morning Herald*, 22 March 2013
18. Annual *Readers Digest* Survey
19. www.exploredia.com, forbes.com, ntdv.com, ufcw1167.org/news
20. OECD Better Life Index, www.probonoaustralia.com.au, 29 May 2013
21. http://www.theguardian.com/business/2014/jan/oxfam-85-richest, by Graeme Wearden
22. www.smh.com.au/opinion/politics/hey-rich-list-its-payback-time, 8 March 2012
23. Lawler, Simon, *AM*, ABC, September 2008
24. weknowmemes.com.tag/teaching-the-only-profession-where-you-steal-supplies-from-home
25. Beuttner, Dan, *Thrive*

5

1. *Education Horizons, Journal of Excellence in Teaching*, Vol. 12, No. 2, 2012, reference survey Parent–Teacher Partnership
2. www.ministers.deewr.gov.au, report commissioned by the Family–school Partnership Bureau and the Australian Council of State Schools Organisation
3. PISA in Brief; Highlights from the full Australian Report; 2012 ACER
4. Rimm, S.B., *Underachievement Syndrome: Causes and Cures*, p. 303–307
5. Huffington, Arianna, *Thrive*, p. 149
6. Edwards, Ben, *Growing Up In Australia*
7. *Sunday Times*, Singapore, 29 April 2012
8. www.goenglish.com/Burning The Candle At Both Ends
9. www.abc.net.au/news 24, October 2012, Sydney University Study by Brigid van Wanrooy
10. www.dailymercury.com.au, 5 December 2011
11. Peacock, Barbara, Centre for Work and Life, University of South Australia
12. Ibid.
13. Ripley, Amanda, *The Smartest Kids in the World and How They Got That Way*, 2013
14. Woods, Judith, 'A Virtual Obsession', *The Daily Telegraph*, 26 April 2013
15. Massachusetts Institute of Technology
16. Greenfield, Susan, Director of

the Institute for the Future of the Mind, Oxford University.
17. Sydney Myopia Study, Brien Holden Vision Institute, University of NSW, reported in *Sun Herald*, 23 August 2015
18. Hinkley, Trina, Healthy Active Preschool Years (HAPPY study)
19. Highfield, Kate, Institute of Early Childhood, Macquarie University
20. Walker, Richard & Mike Horsley, Reforming Homework Practices, Learning and Policies, www.news.com.au/news/should-our-kids-be-doing-homework
21. www.smh.au/national/education
22. www.topicalteaching.com, 21 September 2011

6

1. Sahlberg, Pasi, *Finnish Lessons*, p. 140
2. Ibid., p. 75
3. Ibid., p. 144
4. Ibid., p. 36
5. Ibid., p. 9
6. Ibid., p. 92
7. Ibid., p. 11
8. Ibid., p. 144
9. Ibid., p. 65
10. Ibid., p. 26
11. Ibid., p. 132
12. Ibid., p. 10
13. Ibid., p. 59
14. Ibid., p. 44
15. Ibid., p. 113
16. Ibid., p. 40
17. Ibid., p. 143
18. Ibid., p. 120
19. Ibid., p. 100
20. Ibid., p. 101
21. Ibid., p. 105
22. Haataien, Tuulan, Education Minister of Finland, 30 January 2012
23. http://teacherleaders.typepad.com, 25 May, 2011

Conclusion

1. Sahlberg, Pasi, *Finnish Lessons*, p. 99
2. www.we-feed-the-world.at/en/film.htm
3. Patel, Taj, *The Value of Nothing*, p. 78
4. Connell, Raewin, University of Sydney, *Sydney Morning Herald*, 17 March 2012
5. www.mediadecoder.blogs.com
6. www.hollywoodreporter.com/news, 18 May 2013
7. *Fighting for Equality in Education*, Save Our Schools, 14 March 2011
8. Heliemann, Joel www.nymag.com/news/intelligencer
9. www.huffingtonpost.com, 8 April 2013
10. www.bbc.co.uk/news/technology, 6 March 2013
11. Wolfe, Alan, www.nytimes.com Sunday Book Review, 2010
12. Sahlberg, op. cit. p. 125
13. Sahlberg, op. cit. p. 57
14. Sahlberg, op. cit. p. 128
15. Charlton, Andrew, 'Dragon's Tail', *Quarterly Essay*, Issue 54, 2014
16. Dennis, Richard & Matt Grudnoff, The Australia Institute, *The Conversation*, 15 May 2013
17. Cleary, Paul, *Too Much Luck*, p. 94
18. Ibid., p. 83

19. Gonski Fact Sheet, AEU, 2012
20. Dewan, Sabina & Michael Ettinger, *Comparing Public Spending and Priorities Across OECD Countries*, Centre for American Progress, 2009
21. Education At a Glance, OECD, www.news.com, 13 September 2011
22. Bonner, Chris, opinion piece, www.nationaltimes.com.au
23. www.igiveagonski.com, 2013
24. Wikipedia
25. PISA in Brief: Highlights from the full Australian report, 2012
26. Bantick, Christopher, opinion piece, 27 November 2012
27. Crosby, Robert, *Australian Education Voice Journal*, November 2012
28. Wikipedia.org/wiki/program For International Student Assessment
29. Wikipedia.org/wiki/PISA, 29 May 2013
30. http://www.oecd.org/newsroom/asian-countries-top-oecd-latest-pisa-survey, 3 December 2013
31. http://www.oecdorg/pisa
32. Tarrant, Louise, Divided We Stand: Why Inequality Keeps Rising, 8 March 2012
33. Leigh, Andrew, *Battlers and Billionaires*, Black Inc, 2013
34. Ali, Waleed, *Quarterly Essay*, Issue 37, 2010, p. 31
35. ABC *Lateline*, reporter Melissa Clarke, 11 June 2014
36. Sahlberg, Pasi, op. cit. p. 95
37. www.theguardian.com/education/2014/jul/15/headteacher-noto-pupils-viral-lanc
38. Gavrielatos, Angelo, AEU, 6 December 2012
39. OECD Better Life Index, www.adelaidenow.com.au
40. www.abs.gov.au/ausstats, July 2014
41. Menezes, Flavio, Professor of Economics, Queensland University, *The Conversation*, 13 June 2014
42. Chartlon, Andrew, op. cit. p. 36
43. www.asrc.org.au/media/
44. www.abc.net.au/news, 12 May 2013, source: Asylum Seeker Resource Centre and Parliamentary Library of Australia
45. *Canberra Times*, May 2013

Bibliography

Abey, Arun & Ford, Andrew, *How Much Is Enough?*, A&B Publishers, 2008
Beuttner, Dan, *Thrive*, National Geographic, 2008
Bolte-Taylor, Jill, *My Stroke Of Insight*, Hodder & Stoughton, 2008
Bonner, Chris & Jane Caro, *The Stupid Country*, University of New South Wales Press, 2007
Canfield, Jack, *Chicken Soup For the Teacher's Soul*, Health Communications, 1999
Cheatum, Billye & Allison Hammond, *Physical Activities For Improving Children's Learning and Behaviour*
Cleary, Paul, *Too Much Luck*, 2000
Doidge, Norman, *The Brain That Changes Itself*, Scribe, 2007
Eady, Julie, *Additive Alert*, Additive Alert Publications, 2004
Goddard, Sally, *Reflexes, Learning and Behaviour*, Fern Ridge Press, 2005
Gold, Svea, *If Kids Just Came With Instruction Sheets*, Fern Ridge Press, 1997
Goleman, Daniel, *Emotional Intelligence*, Bloomsbury, 1996
—. *Social Intelligence*, Hutchinson, 2006
Gopnik, Alison, Andrew Meltzofi & Patricia Kuhl, *The Scientist In the Crib*, Harper Perennial, 2001
Hannaford, Carla, Smart Moves: *Why Learning Is Not All in Your Head*, Great River Books, 2005
Patel, Raj, *The Value of Nothing*, Black Inc, 2010
Pheloung, Barbara, *Help Your Child To Learn*, Iceform Pty Ltd, 2004
—, *Help Your Class To Learn*, Barbara Pheloung, 1997
—, *Overcoming Learning Difficulties*, Doubleday, 1992
—, *School Floors*, Iceform Pty Ltd, 2006
Robinson, Ken with Lou Aronica, *The Element*, Allan Lane, 2009
Sahlberg, Pasi, *Finnish Lessons*, Hawker Brownlow Education, 2012
Siegel, Dan, *Mindsight: Change Your Brain and Your Life*, Scribe, 2009

www.ingramcontent.com/pod-product-compliance
Lightning Source LLC
Chambersburg PA
CBHW070101120526
44589CB00033B/1325